BACKSTREET BOYS

BOYS

Official Biography

Rob McGibbon

B⬛XTREE

First published in 1997 by Boxtree, an imprint of Macmillan
Publishers Ltd, 25 Eccleston Place, London, SW1W 9NF and
Basingstoke

Associated companies throughout the world

ISBN 0 7522 2406 9

Front cover design by Blackjacks
Picture credits: © The Backstreet Boys

9 8 7 6

A CIP catalogue record for this book is available from the British
Library

Typeset by SX Composing DTP, Rayleigh, Essex
Printed by Mackays of Chatham PLC, Kent

CONTENTS

ACKNOWLEDGEMENTS

I was lucky to have the kind help of many people in different parts of America while researching this book. Sadly, it is impossible to name them all, but certain people deserve a special acknowledgement.

In Lexington, I would like to thank Alicia at the Porter Memorial Church where it all began; Dave and Chris Cawood for their time and photographs; Ben McNees, David Blanton and all Brian's teachers. In Irvine: thanks to Dwaine and Dena Riddell; Shawn Jones, Christi Ore, Hoover Niece, and to Rita Durbin, Andy and Cindy Sigmon at Cathedral Domain. In Orlando: to Greg Carswell, Dirk Donahue, Gersh Morningstar, and to Scott Hoekstra for his candidness. I am also grateful to British Airways for an unbeatable first class service to America.

Many people in the Backstreet Boys organisation have been extremely helpful and I'm grateful to Nicole Peltz, Bob Fischetti, road manager Nina Bueti and particularly to Denise McLean, the wonderful Mama of the tours.

Special thanks must go to the Backstreet Boys – AJ, Howie, Nick, Kevin and Brian for their openness and honesty. You deserve to go all the way, guys, and here's to that platinum. Above all, my thanks to the irrepressible Lou Pearlman for asking me to write this fascinating story.

Praise must go to Adrian Sington and to my editor Clare Hulton at Boxtree who showed unwavering belief in this book long before most people had even heard of the Backstreet Boys. Sincere thanks also to my agent Jonathan Lloyd for his work and valuable advice.

On a personal note, I would like to thank all my family for their constant support in everything.

Rob McGibbon 7 April 1997

INTRODUCTION

Work on this biography began in Lexington, Kentucky, where I researched the early lives of Brian Littrell and Kevin Richardson. From there, I went to Irvine, in the wild countryside of the state, for further information on Kevin's time at Cathedral Domain, his home in the hills. The next stage took me to Orlando, Florida, where I travelled extensively, piecing together the early years of AJ McLean, Howie Dorough and Nick Carter. In all of the towns I conducted dozens of interviews with the boys' close childhood friends, teachers, singing tutors and their first girlfriends to gain an insight into all facets of their lives. I also traced the key people who helped the Backstreet Boys before they were famous, as well as one of the original members of the band who quit. All that research was for an unofficial biography. Then I met Lou Pearlman.

Lou is a millionaire businessman and the creator of the Backstreet Boys: he discovered them, bankrolled their formative years and, against the odds, turned them into pop stars. Although now 42, Lou is widely considered to be the Sixth member of the group. He was so amazed by the depth of my research that, over dinner in Orlando, he asked me to write the Official Book, which is when Phase Two began.

I travelled to Belgium and Sweden in February 1997 to watch the Backstreet Boys on their European tour. I saw virtually every dimension of their lives as teen heart throbs. I saw them relaxing backstage, in their hotels, on the road, and, best of all, I saw their concerts up close and witnessed the fan mania which is growing by the day worldwide. During this period, I interviewed the boys and Lou extensively. They spoke openly about their earliest childhood memories, their sad experiences, their first days as performers, the tough days trying to make it, and about life today in the slipstream of stardom.

This book is the result of those interviews, plus all the other original material. Thanks to two different dimensions of research, it is without question the only biography to tell the whole story of the group. It is a detailed and honest account which reveals how five boys from varying backgrounds rose from obscurity to the dizzy heights of fame. The story begins with the fateful day in New York when Lou Pearlman first had the idea to start a pop group . . .

1

THE DREAM BELIEVER

Lou Pearlman has a simple saying to sum up his philosophy in life: *If you can dream it, you can do it.*

It is an attitude he has applied to everything since he was a little boy. Whenever he longed to do something he found a way, whatever the barriers or the risks, and regardless of the doubters who said it couldn't be done. This unshakeable self-belief helped him rise from humble beginnings to become a multi-millionaire and head of an international business empire.

But, more importantly, Lou's drive shaped the destiny of five young men and turned their wild dreams of pop stardom into stunning reality with the Backstreet Boys.

It started with an everyday conversation in the summer of 1989, as Lou sat in his cousin's luxury apartment overlooking New York's Central Park. His cousin is no ordinary man. He is Art Garfunkel, half of the legendary duet Simon and Garfunkel, who had a series of hits throughout the 1960s and '70s, including the classic 'Bridge Over Troubled Water'. Art's mum and Lou's dad were sister and brother and the families were always very close.

Lou is 12 years younger than his cousin, and he watched in awe through his teenage years as Art became a music icon. Witnessing the success and adulation Art enjoyed sparked a deep passion inside Lou for music and the exciting world of rock 'n' roll which would never fade.

He tried his own hand at the guitar and had some modest success in the 1970s in a little known band called Flyer, which opened for acts including Barry White and Kool and the Gang. He was also a producer and had written many songs, but he gave up dreams of following in his famous cousin's chord riffs when he realised it wasn't paying the bills. As Lou puts it, he got a serious day job. He concentrated on an area where he showed genuine brilliance – business. And it paid off. He was a naturally gifted entrepreneur who could take a simple idea and turn it into a thriving success. In 15 years he rose from a college boy without a cent in the bank to become a seriously wealthy businessman.

But, despite all the money and success, Lou still had a fascination for the music business, so it's not surprising he listened a little bit more closely when Art started talking about the current music scene that evening eight years ago. Art had been amazed by the rise of the New Kids on the Block, who were on his own record label, Columbia. New Kids hysteria was the topic of news bulletins around the world and it reminded Art of the scenes which followed The Beatles in the '60s and the Osmonds in the '70s, as well as his own experiences. Was it all cyclical, he wondered?

Like any true entrepreneur, Lou's mind is forever turning over ideas and trying to focus on the next big thing. His sixth sense started to stir during that conversation and, long after they had moved on to other subjects, it was still ticking. By the time Lou walked out into the muggy New York summer night, his mind was buzzing with possibilities. The seed that would grow into the Backstreet Boys had been sown.

Lou had already heard of the New Kids because his aviation company provided private jets for their tours, but he had never thought of them as more than one name among dozens of celebrity clients. But now he was interested in them and resolved to find out what all the fuss was about. A few months later, he was standing among thousands of screaming girls at the Nassau Coliseum arena, just outside New York City, and his questions were answered. The whole event blew his mind.

Lou had just turned 35 and stuck out like the proverbial sore thumb among the hoards of teenagers, but he wasn't bothered. He was as mesmerised as the young fans by the charisma and energy of Donnie Wahlberg and his pals and the frenzy they whipped up in the arena. The New Kids weren't being hailed as gifted song writers, or amazingly talented singers, but they were undoubtedly brilliant showmen. Girls screamed themselves to the brink of exhaustion and scores were carried out by security men. It was an intoxicating atmosphere and Lou loved every second.

As he left that night, his ears were buzzing and his mind was racing. The New Kids were not only an exhilarating stage act, they were also a thriving multi-million pound business, gilt-edged with all the excitement and fun of the music industry. It was the perfect combination for an ageing failed rocker with a young heart and a mature business brain. His heart had always been with music, but his head belonged in business. He couldn't help wondering, Wouldn't it be fantastic to have your own pop group?

There was another, more poignant, factor which motivated Lou to start what would become the Backstreet Boys: he desperately wanted a family. He was an only child and had recently begun to feel very alone in the world after losing both his parents. His father, Herman – or Hy, as everyone knew him – had died in 1982 and his mother, Reenie, had died on Mother's Day in 1988. Losing them had left him devastated and his loss was compounded because he didn't have a family of his own and there seemed little chance of him settling down. He had been involved in two serious relationships but, for various reasons, particularly his commitment to work, they hadn't worked out. Although Lou had many good friends and an extended family in his business empire, it wasn't the same. He felt that starting a young group and nurturing their dreams could be the next best thing to having his own children.

It would be two and a half years before Lou actively began his search for the next teen sensation, but the idea continually bounced around his head. He kept a sharp eye on the New Kids' phenomenal development and arranged for a complimentary copy of their platinum album *Hangin' Tough* to be sent to him from Columbia. Typically shrewd, he didn't buy one.

Shortly after moving from New York to Florida in 1991, he went to another concert at the Orlando Arena and this time he came away determined to put his ideas into practice. He told close friends and some business associates what he was going to do and the common reaction was that he had gone mad.

'I was completely knocked out by the New Kids,' says Lou. 'I had been really interested ever since Art mentioned them to me and I couldn't get them out of my mind. I loved the energy and it was fascinating to see so many kids attach themselves to the band – it was almost like a cult.'

But Lou had a dream and he was going to make it come true. It would take four long years, a gamble of more than £1 million, and the unbreakable dedication of five boys before it would even begin to come into focus. To understand why Lou never gave up, despite countless disappointments, and why the Backstreet Boys all acknowledge him for their success, it is important to know a little more about the sixth Backstreet Boy, the man they all call Big Poppa.

Louis J. Pearlman was born on 19 June 1954 and spent much of his childhood in Flushing, a suburb in the district of Queens, around 20 miles from the skyscrapers of Manhattan. The Pearlmans were not a wealthy family. His dad had run a successful laundry business in Brooklyn, which had been handed down through the family, but the shop was burnt down during riots and was not covered by insurance. Hy had to start from scratch and became a driver for another laundry company, making what he could from delivery charges and tips. Money was tight so Reenie supplemented their income by working at a local school.

Although they were far from being on the bread line, there was little room for luxuries. Lou never went without, but if he wanted anything extra, he had to work for it. This led to his first business venture at the age of eight, when he hit on the classic money-spinning idea of making lemonade and selling it to his friends and neighbours. It was a typically sweltering New York summer and Lou was certain he could sell gallons of his home-made drink. He calculated it would cost two cents a glass to make and could be sold for five cents and the profits would pour in. Well, he was half right.

Sure enough, the lemonade went down sweetly and his pockets filled up with change, but the bubble of Lou's lemonade idea burst when the day's accounting showed he had *lost* money. He was angry and puzzled. How could he have worked so hard for nothing? He soon realised the reason: he had drunk the profits. He had willingly joined his customers in a drink and, therefore, had not taken enough money to cover the expenses of the ingredients. He now knew the difference between gross profit and net profit and, although it was a bitter lesson to swallow, it was one he would never forget.

Lou's next entrepreneurial enterprise was far more successful. He started a paper delivery round, but wasn't enamoured of the physical graft or the black newsprint stains on his hands and arms. He hit on a solution: Why not pay a younger lad to do the round for him and take a cut of his wages? That way he would earn money without having to lift so much as one newspaper. It was a great idea and before long, Lou had secured nine rounds and was responsible for organising all the delivery boys and all the wages. It was so successful that he linked up with a local baker to add fresh bagels and bread deliveries to his operation. From every delivery, Lou took a small cut. It was clear that the little boy had a natural talent for running a business and a sharp mind for finance.

When he was 10, Lou was awe-struck by the sight of the giant Goodyear Tyre airship – or 'blimp' as they are known in America – which was based at the Flushing airport and had turned millions of heads skywards during the World Trade Fair. Never lacking confidence or cheek, Lou went to the airport and asked the Goodyear ground crew if he could have a ride. The answer was an emphatic No because company rules stipulated that only relatives of employees or journalists qualified for a trip. Quick as a flash, Lou said: 'That's great. I can have a ride because I write for my school newspaper.'

Technically, he was not supposed to ride in the airship, but he talked the crew round and watched open-mouthed as it hummed thousands of feet above the Manhattan skyline. From that day, he was hooked and became what is known in the airship world as a 'helium head'. Little more than 15 years later, airships would help make Lou rich and give him the resources to create the Backstreet Boys.

The critical idea which put Lou on the path to riches came when he was 21 and studying for a business degree at Queens College. To get by, he worked as an airship ground crewman at Teterboro Airport after Flushing had closed. As part of his college course he was required to think up a new business specifically for New York and present a detailed plan analysing its viability and profit potential. While working at the airport, Lou had noticed how executives who flew in on private jets were picked up by limousine to face a long journey through heavy traffic to Manhattan. Lou couldn't understand why they didn't use helicopters, which would take a fraction of the time. He mentioned the idea of a shuttle service to the East Side of the Hudson River to his workmates, who dismissed it bluntly. 'If it was a good idea, somebody would be doing it already,' they said. But Lou was not deterred. He had belief in the idea and produced a detailed projection which his course professor greeted positively. He gave Lou an A-grade and was certain it had genuine merit, not just in theory.

Lou completed his studies, earning a Masters degree and a PhD in business, and then focused on the reality of making money. He convinced several people, including two of his lecturers and his uncle Jack Garfunkel, to invest in the helicopter idea. It got off to a flying start and within a year it had built up £1 million turnover with a client list of top businessmen and celebrities. Lou began to think of fresh angles to exploit the helicopter transportation market and one great idea followed another, such as flying large cheques direct from international airports to the Federal Reserve Bank on Wall Street. A speedy delivery ensured a valuable day's interest for the bank and a large fee for Lou's company.

Lou eventually sold the helicopter business to start Trans Continental Airlines, which leased private jets to the rich and famous and various commercial enterprises, including cargo delivery and tourist flights to Las Vegas. By the time he was 28, Lou was a multi-millionaire and had bought the first of three Rolls Royces. The aviation company had many branches and it had expanded into one crucial area – airships, the machines which had captivated his imagination as a boy. Lou's brilliance for exploiting gaps in the market struck again when he began hiring out his airships for advertising. It was a stroke of genius and soon he was running one of the biggest airship businesses in the world, with clients such as

McDonald's, Budweiser and even the rock group Pink Floyd, as well as major TV companies who would lease his airships for sporting event coverage. Airships became the backbone of the company, and in 1984 Lou's company was floated on the Stock Exchange and over the years raised £20 million.

The little helium head from Flushing was now wealthy beyond his dreams, but Lou's appetite for new challenges never waned. Luckily for five young boys, he then decided to try his Midas touch in the music business.

Lou's aim was to emulate the approach taken by music producer Maurice Starr, who plucked five boys from the streets of Boston and groomed them into the New Kids on the Block. There were two distinct differences in Lou's approach. Firstly, he wanted a group with strong voices. The New Kids had come under scathing criticism for their vocal limitations, so Lou made talent a priority because it would secure firmer foundations for longer-lasting success. Secondly, he would search for his stars of the future in the Sunshine State, Florida.

Lou had settled in Orlando, the vibrant home of tourism and entertainment on the East Coast of the United States, and it seemed the perfect place to find boys with talent. Orlando already boasted Disney World and it was fast becoming America's second Hollywood, thanks to the arrival of Universal and MGM movie studios. The city had a busy circuit of working young actors and singers and its drama schools were bursting with potential. All Lou needed was a way of tapping into that talent.

The first person he turned to was Gloria Sicoli, the wife of one of his oldest friends, Frank, who now worked for him. Gloria was a singer with years of experience in the record business. During the 1980s, she was in an all-girl group, which had enjoyed some chart success, and had secured her a solo recording contract with RCA. Sadly, things didn't work out, but Gloria continued as a successful backing singer with a number of top American pop acts. She had seen the good and the downright nasty side of the record industry and Lou realised her knowledge was invaluable. Furthermore, Gloria was working as an actress at Universal Studios, as well as teaching drama at the Civic Theater of Central Florida. She had her finger on the pulse of the Orlando entertainment scene so, in June 1992, Lou asked her to be the talent scout for his new venture. She enthusiastically took up the challenge.

Gloria's first step was to print some fly sheets and place ads in the *Sentinel*, Orlando's main daily newspaper, and the *Florida Blue Sheet*, an entertainment trade paper equivalent to the *Stage* in Britain. The ads read: *Teen male vocalists. Producer seeks male teen singers that move well between 16–19 years of age. Wanted for New Kids-type singing/dance group. Send photo or bio' of any kind to . . .*

Gloria clearly remembers those first days.

'After Lou called me, I spent about a month scouting before we did any auditions. I got the ads published and put up flyers in all the high schools and drama schools around Orlando. I did a lot of the work on foot and even put flyers under car windscreens and in shop windows. I put them anywhere that would get the idea talked about. Although we said we wanted a New Kids-type group, Lou didn't want to produce a clone, but we had to narrow it down, so the guys knew what we were after.

'I started going to all kinds of theatre shows and auditions that were being held for young guys. I would sit in the back row and watch everybody and pick out the ones I liked to come and audition. I spotted some talented guys and there was a good response from the ads, so Lou and I started holding auditions at his house during July.

'I operated a video camera while Lou watched them sing and dance. We wanted guys who looked good and could sing and dance well. Above all, we wanted guys with nice personalities, who were team players, not kids with big ego problems. We auditioned a lot of boys, but couldn't find exactly what we wanted.

'I kept scouting around and started going through the archives at the Civic Theatre where there were thousands of head shots of young performers and a summary of the entertainment work they had done. I picked out a batch of about a dozen, but two guys really stuck out. They looked great and had plenty of experience.'

One of the boys Gloria liked was Alexander James McLean and the other was Tony Donetti.

2

TALL STORIES FROM DOPEY

It was Saturday, 1 August and Alex, or AJ as he would become known, was the first on Gloria's audition list. He was due at 12.30 and would be followed by Tony Donetti at 2.30. It was clear from the promotion photos that they both had dark, handsome looks and were already seasoned performers with plenty of singing, dancing and acting experience. Gloria and Lou had a good feeling the boys would prove more suitable than the others they had interviewed. And they weren't disappointed.

AJ arrived with his mum, Denise, who chaperoned her son to most auditions. They had heard about Lou Pearlman's wealth and his airship company and, as they pulled off International Drive to his beautiful home, it was clear the stories of his success had not been exaggerated. Although not ostentatious, it is a big four-bedroom house and the two Rolls Royces and stretch limousine didn't look out of place in the drive. (Lou's third Rolls is kept at his other home in New York.) It was obvious to Alex and Denise that if this guy was serious about launching a pop group, he would easily have the finances.

Further evidence of Lou's wealth and, more importantly, his character was on view inside the house. In a glass case was one of the four original C-3PO gold robot costumes from the *Star Wars* blockbuster movie; in another was the helmet worn by arch villain Darth Vader; by the bar in the vast lounge area was one of the original models of the USS Enterprise from the *Star Trek* films. These

10

are highly valuable ornaments, but apart from the money, it shows that when Lou Pearlman is passionate about something he doesn't do things by half measures. He makes sure he gets the best money can buy, and once he has his possession, he gives it the best care possible. As Lou puts it, he has 'precious feelings' towards his investments and always makes sure they are looked after. This would be the premise with which he would handle the Backstreet Boys.

AJ and Denise were instantly charmed by Lou. He appeared more like a friendly uncle than the boss of a big company and AJ was pleasantly surprised. He says: 'I was expecting some tough guy businessman in a suit. But Lou was laid back and very friendly. I thought, Hey, this guy is real cool. I liked him immediately and I could tell he was serious about the group. It wasn't just some passing fad.'

AJ had to sing one of three New Kids songs – 'I'll Be Loving You Forever', 'Didn't I Blow Your Mind' or 'Please Don't Go Girl'. The song was chosen at random and then he sang to a backing tape, while Gloria videoed him and Lou watched with Denise from a couch. AJ was then asked to dance in any style to a piece of music of his choice. To look at, he was just a wiry little boy of 14 back then, but appearances were deceptive. He had a lively character and the self-confidence of a boy many years older and he came alive when he performed. He had wonderful natural dance rhythm, which had been honed with tuition, and a powerful voice which showed promise of developing into a full baritone. On top of this, he had striking stage presence for one so young. In short, he was perfect for a pop group.

But what Lou and Gloria saw that Saturday would not have surprised anyone who knew AJ, especially his mum.

Denise McLean knew from her only child's earliest years that he was an extrovert who sought attention exhaustively. AJ was born on 9 January 1978 and even as a toddler he was an energetic and amusing little showman, who would dance around and entertain friends and family. He was rarely happier than when he was the focus of attention. As he grew older, he would sing for anyone who cared to listen and showed an uncanny talent for mimicking the people he met, whether they were neighbours or characters he saw on television. AJ admits that at times he was unbearably demanding. It is a characteristic he largely puts down to the emotional upheaval of his parents' bitter marriage break-up. AJ was only five when his mum and dad, Robert, separated, and Denise was left to bring up AJ alone, while his father disappeared from their lives. Robert played no part in his son's childhood. He didn't call or write and had no contact except for a fleeting Christmas visit when AJ was 10 years old. Only years later, when AJ was enjoying success with the Backstreet Boys, would his father finally come back into his life and the two men would build a relationship.

Thanks to her parents' constant support, Denise was able to work to provide a comfortable and secure home for AJ. They lived on a new housing estate in Boynton Beach, a small coastal town near West Palm Beach, 70 or so miles from Miami. It was a pretty part of Florida for a young boy to grow up and AJ had an active childhood. Although he had a loving home, he admits the turmoil of his parents' divorce had a major affect on him and, at times, it was confusing growing up without a dad around.

'My father was never around when I was a kid and it was pretty tough on me. He never wrote and I never got any birthday cards or anything. I would watch the other kids go out and play basketball or baseball with their dads, but I never had that.

'We never spoke about my dad around the house, so I never really got to understand why he left us. I think one of the reasons I craved so much attention was because my dad wasn't around. With him gone, I needed to make sure I got all the attention I could from everyone else. But, even though I didn't have a dad, I had a great childhood. I got all the love and support I needed. My mom and my grandparents were fantastic and I owe everything to them. They were always there for me and supported me in everything I wanted to do. They gave me the security I needed in my life. Without them, who knows how I would have turned out.'

Ironically, it was the absence of his father which ultimately helped shape AJ's future as a pop star. Denise had always been interested in acting and the entertainment business generally and when she saw AJ's natural flair for performing, she was eager to help him pursue it. After seeing an advert in a local newspaper seeking kids for a fashion show at the Boca Raton shopping mall, she put AJ forward. He was only seven, but he got the job and was a confident natural on the catwalk – or 'runway', as it is known in America. It would prove to be the launch pad that put AJ on an upward trajectory to stardom.

AJ remembers his first tentative step into the world of showbiz well.

'My mom noticed I was a natural ham – I loved attention and I would do anything just to make sure I got it. I was always talking and would drive my grandparents mad. I would talk their ears off until they couldn't hear me anymore and dance around making sure everyone was looking at me. When I was a little kid, my cousin and I would do skits of things we had seen on the television. I just loved everyone looking at me and laughing.

'The fashion show was the first proper thing I did and I loved it. Everyone thought I might be a bit nervous because all the other kids were so much older, but I had a great time. I had to change in the same room at the back with the older female models. There I was, just seven years old, and these tall beautiful women were stripping in front of me. I couldn't believe what I was seeing – I was in awe. They thought I was cute and they pampered me.'

Another woman watching in the audience thought AJ was cute, too. She liked his cheeky grin and was impressed by his confidence. Her name was Nona Lloyd, and she knew from experience when a child had natural ability on the stage. Nona was the director of the local children's musical theatre and organised productions at the Royal Palm Dinner Theater in Delray, the next town a few miles along the coast. Dinner theatres offer an entertainment package where people tuck into a meal while watching a stage production. Nona was always on the lookout for new talent and was now searching for little boys to play dwarfs in a production of *Snow White*. The show was due to run for a month at weekends, but she was having problems finding enough youngsters. When she saw AJ she knew he would be perfect.

'Nona got talking to my mum and I went down and auditioned for her at the theatre. She liked me but wasn't sure if my skills were up to par for a speaking part. I hadn't done any acting before, but she felt I could handle the role of Dopey because he doesn't have to say a word. It was a fantastic break for me.

'When the show opened I was very nervous, but also really excited. I'd learnt a bit of sign language for my scenes but I didn't really understand what I was doing. I was the comic relief character and got everyone laughing. I couldn't believe the reaction I got because it was all so new to me. I was just being myself and it was working. I don't mean to be conceited, but I stole the show and I loved every second of it.

'After the opening night, I got my first taste of being sort of famous. A lot of kids came up and asked me for my autograph. I couldn't really believe it, but it was great. I signed my full name for them – Alexander James McLean. It was really cool. I enjoyed doing that show so much and I remember having the biggest crush on the girl who played Snow White. She must have been 10 years older than me, but to this day I remember her.'

The youngsters in the audience were thrilled by AJ's performance and so was Doc Peterson, the manager of the theatre, and the man AJ remembers fondly as the 'head honcho'. Doc had overall responsibility for all the shows and he was so impressed with the little newcomer playing Dopey that he quickly signed him up for the next production. And this time AJ got a speaking part.

It was the start of a long and successful career in children's theatre and AJ went on to perform in 27 productions. He grew in confidence and ability and gradually worked his way up from minor walk-on parts to lead roles. He loved to be on stage with a thousand or more people watching his every move and during his years performing in theatre he gradually saw the possibility of a professional future in the entertainment business. His mum was keen for him to develop his talents and booked him singing and piano lessons. He also became enthusiastic about dancing, his favourite of all performance disciplines, and won a scholarship to the Boca Raton Dance Studio. There he had expert coaching in all forms of dance from ballet to jazz and tap. It would prove to be perfect grounding for his future.

'Dancing was really my thing in the early days,' says AJ. 'I wanted to be a dancer way above an actor or a singer. I could really lose myself while I was dancing – I loved the energy and the freedom. I was acting, dancing and singing and playing the piano right through my childhood. I was always busy doing something and my mum was right there encouraging and helping me all the way. She would chase me to prepare for auditions and she would take me everywhere I needed to go. She boosted me up when I was down and she helped me learn my lines. As long as my heart was set on something, she backed me.'

Alongside his burgeoning career, AJ worked hard at his junior high school and was a good student. The school arranged private tutors if he ever had to miss lessons for matinee performances. When he was not performing, AJ did the normal things young boys do. He hung out with a close bunch of friends on the sweeping beaches at Delray and Boynton. They fooled around local shopping malls on their bikes, played with radio controlled cars and regularly tucked into AJ's favourite meal at McDonald's.

Unfortunately, AJ had a few problems with boys outside his close group.

'A lot of guys made fun of me and gave me a hard time. They would say, "What's your problem, why don't you play basketball like a normal guy?" I tried not to take too much notice, but it was upsetting. To be honest, I think a lot of it was jealousy because they weren't capable of doing the things I was doing and they didn't like the attention I got. I did play sports when I was a kid, but only with my close pals. I didn't have a dad encouraging me, so I wasn't totally committed to sport. Instead, I had my mom saying, "Come on, AJ, time for singing lessons, or piano tuition." The guys I didn't get on with would laugh when they heard I was going for singing lessons.

'I was a bit of a nerd at school and was always a little bit different from the others. All the kids had a knapsack for their school books and a lunch box. I had to be different, so I had a briefcase for my books and kept my lunch in a paper bag. For some crazy reason I saw myself as a little businessman. For a while I wore glasses, even though my eyesight was perfect, because I thought they looked cool. I guess I have always been a bit wacky.'

Apart from the jibes, there was another down side to AJ's love of performing: he had developed a bad habit of lying. It was just another attention seeking device, but it was something which worried his mum and drove her, as well as some of his friends, to distraction. It even cost him his first childhood sweetheart, as he admits.

'I was always a big story teller and it got me into all kinds of trouble. My excuse was that I had an over-active imagination and I loved to express it, but the truth is I was a big liar. I would exaggerate stories to get attention, but I went so far over the top that they became complete fantasy.

'I would elaborate on the truth until it became a total lie. I got completely caught up in telling stories and making things up. I would start talking about something that had happened to me, say at school, and by the time I had finished I would have blown the heck out of the truth. My mom or my grandparents would say, "Now come on, AJ, tell us what really happened." Instead of stopping and holding up my hands, I would come up with more lies to make the story more believable. I couldn't stop myself. I wasn't intending to lie, I just got carried away and loved the fantasy. My first girlfriend dumped me because I lied so much. She was the first person to ever come straight out and call me a liar. I was really hurt, but she was right.'

Despite being dropped that time for his tall stories, AJ never went short of attention from girls throughout his school days. Unlike the sports-mad boys, girls were impressed with his singing and dancing skills, and he was rarely without an innocent childhood sweetheart. But not even the prettiest girls in the class could compete with the woman who captured his heart when he was 11: Paula Abdul. When she released her new single 'Opposites Attract' in 1989, it sparked a burning crush that still flickers today. AJ watched the world premiere of the video, in which Paula sings to a cheeky cartoon tom-cat, and he was in love. He says: 'I know what it's like to be a fan. I was besotted with Paula Abdul for years – I still am! I wanted to marry her from the first day I saw her. When that song came out I thought it was the coolest thing ever. I loved the way she moved and she inspired me to keep dancing. That was my favourite video at the time and the tom-cat got me into drawing cartoons.'

When he was 12, AJ and his mum moved more than 300 miles north to Kissimmee, a town south of Orlando. As a multi-talented child performer, it was crucial for AJ to be near the hub of Orlando where there are countless work opportunities in theatre, TV and the movies, and if a youngster wants to break into show business he has to be where the work is. Denise was as determined as AJ that he should maximise his talents, so he got an agent and quickly joined the treadmill of auditions around the city, with her or his grandmother as his personal chauffeur. AJ had more advanced acting, singing and dancing tuition to prepare him for those readings and screen tests.

Virtually every week, AJ would go up for one job or another and almost every time he would be up against several hundred other boys going for the same part with him. There were countless rejections in those early days, but it was good experience for him to see the tough side of the entertainment world. He got several good breaks with parts in TV shows on Nickelodeon and the Disney Channel and appeared in a Muppets commercial.

His main interest was still dancing and, away from the professional circuit, he started his own dance troupe with two girls and another boy. Their various parents took turns to drive them to competitions around Florida. Although they never won, they worked hard at their routines and, again, it was valuable experience.

Denise and AJ's new home in Kissimmee was a modest flat on a smart development complex called The Polos, and he went to the Denn John Middle School nearby. He may have been the new boy from out of town, but it wasn't long before his singing helped him make his mark. One teacher who was amazed at AJ's abilities was Dirk Donahue, who had just joined as music teacher. He was appalled to see how the school choir had been neglected, so his primary aim was to encourage new talent and build up a singing group the school could be proud of. He decided to hold a talent contest to discover what talent lay untapped in the classrooms. For some reason AJ, who was 13, missed the early auditions, but when he finally found out about the event, he quickly went to sign up. It was a day Mr Donahue remembers well.

'I had never seen Alex before, but I vividly remember our first meeting. He turned up at my classroom and asked to be in the talent show. I had already finished the auditions but, if a guy wants to sing, I let him. Few boys sing, because they think it's girly, so you have to encourage the slightest bit of interest. I said, Sure, Alex, show me what you can do.

'He had a little tape player with him. He popped in a tape with just instrumental music on it and he sang 'Johnny Be Goode' and he knocked my socks off. He had a little dance routine. It was nothing outlandish, but he did a few spins and kept the beat by snapping his fingers. I was pretty amazed by his confidence and he was way ahead of the other kids I had auditioned. I signed him up immediately.

'He was fantastic in the show. He had so much personality and stage presence that it shocked everyone. It was like, Who is this guy? No one seemed to know he could do that. Alex won the competition and beat a girl who had won it two years in a row. He got a trophy and was really excited. You could tell he got a great buzz from performing.'

AJ joined Mr Donahue's choir after his talent show victory and quickly established himself as the leading member. He also landed a part as a sailor in a community theatre production of the musical *South Pacific*, a play Mr Donahue was also appearing in.

'I saw Alex during the day at school and at night for rehearsals. I was really impressed by his dedication. He worked hard in my classes and was by far the most gifted student. He had a great voice but could also sing with expression. Basically, he could sell a song better than the other kids.

'The *South Pacific* production was an adult show. There were only two kids in it – a girl of 13 and Alex. He was working with guys in their twenties, but he wasn't intimidated. In fact, he picked up the choreography quicker than any of them. He had a quicker brain and feet for the steps. He was made to look a bit older with make-up and also doubled up as a native in other scenes. Even back then I thought he could be a star one day. Some people can perform well enough, but they don't necessarily have great stage presence. Alex had it all. He had masses of talent and he could capture an audience. When he was on stage he would just light up.'

AJ briefly attended Osceola High School after Denn John Middle. He quickly shone out in Greg Carswell's choral classes and he put his story-telling talents to good use by entertaining other pupils with ghost stories at Halloween. But one of AJ's biggest triumphs in those formative years came out of school when he was 14 and he entered a talent contest at a Latin Carnival. He spent many hours preparing a mini one-man show, which displayed his acting, singing and dancing talents, as well as the puppetry skills he had developed. It was a complex compilation, but he mastered it brilliantly and won the $1,000 first prize. AJ beat another budding star of the future that day. He was Tony Donetti.

The two boys didn't know each other then but they met at an audition a few weeks after the carnival and Tony congratulated AJ on his win. Although Tony was five years older, they had a lot in common and got on well immediately. They had both spent years acting and singing and had similar Latin looks, so they were going for the same jobs. They kept bumping into each other on the showbiz circuit over the next few months and gradually became good friends.

It was not surprising they were both spotted by Gloria Sicoli, but it was an amazing coincidence that Tony, out of the many Gloria had looked at, should be on her list to follow AJ's audition at Lou Pearlman's house.

However, what no one realised – even AJ – was that Tony Donetti was a stage name for Howie Dorough and that the double identity would nearly cost him his chance of stardom.

3

THE GHOST OF DONETTI

Howie hated his stage name, but his acting agent insisted he adopt it because he felt 'Howie Dorough' was too weak and unmemorable to help him make it as an entertainer. The agent even chose the new name, and when Howie heard its origins he felt uneasy, to say the least. The 'Tony' came from one of the agent's former clients and close friends who had died tragically. The 'Donetti' derived from a character played by one of the agent's heroes, Mario Lanza, a singer and movie star of the 1950s. The amalgamation of names from two dead performers was hardly a good omen. Howie also resented pretending to be something he wasn't, but his agent said he would be more marketable as an Italian. Howie was half Spanish and half Irish, and he felt uncomfortable denying his heritage, but he was 16 when he was first told to change his name and he was desperate to be famous, so he reluctantly agreed. Like the agent, Howie believed 'Tony Donetti' would stay in people's minds and make him famous. How wrong they both were.

Howard Dwaine Dorough was already a competent showman long before he changed his name. He was born in Orlando on 22 August 1973, the last of five children to Hoke and Paula Dorough. Hoke's family was originally from Ireland and Paula was from Puerto Rico, which accounts for Howie's dark looks. Howie was the baby of the family by 10 years. He has three elder sisters: Angie, Caroline, Polly, and an elder brother, Johnny. The family were not well off, but Hoke and Paula worked hard to give their children all they needed. During the day, Hoke worked in the patrol section of the police and he had a job as a security guard at a bank in the evenings. He also worked as a police dog trainer at the weekends, while Paula worked all week in a local school's canteen. The Doroughs knew the value of hard work and Howie grew up learning that discipline. All the children were brought up in a strict Catholic faith and taught that if you want something, you work for it.

Despite his parents' hard work ethic, the Dorough household had a light-hearted and bustling atmosphere. The big age gap between Howie and the rest of the children ensured him all the attention he could possibly wish for. His brother and sisters doted on him and they encouraged him to ham up and sing for them. One of the earliest signs of Howie's extrovert character showed itself at three, when he would gladly sing along for everyone to the chart hit of the moment 'Baby Face', while pretending to strum on a toy guitar. The song had been the only hit for the oddly named group, Wing and a Prayer Fife and Drum Corps. They would vanish into obscurity, but the Dorough family would always remember their song for Howie's performances.

Howie continued to entertain his family, but when he was six his sister Polly felt it was time he tried a bigger stage. Polly was actively involved in school plays and community theatre and while she was rehearsing for a production of *The Wizard of Oz*, she took her little brother along for his first audition. Howie still remembers that day vividly.

'They needed a lot of little kids to play the munchkins and Polly was encouraging me to have a try. I had seen her in plays and musicals before and I loved the idea of getting up on stage. I wanted to do the show, but I was hesitant because I was so shy and didn't know if I could do it.

'I tagged along with Polly and the director guy came round to me and asked me to sing. I didn't want to do it at first, but suddenly I thought, Yeah, I'll have a go. It was the first time I ever sang in the business and the director thought it was great and gave me a part. I was so happy.

Baby Kevin at the family home in Lexington.

Baby Nick, the boy who would become a teen heart throb.

Baby AJ takes a bath.

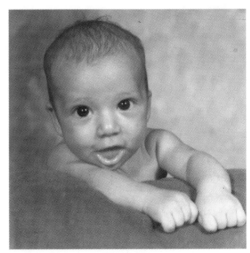

Baby Howie gurgles for the camera.

Brian, aged 12.

Brian, aged 13.

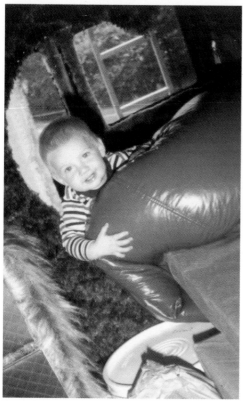

Cheeky Nick, aged two, climbs over the furniture.

Howie, aged five, enjoys Christmas in his Santa romper suit.

Nick's proud grandfather holds his grandson.

Yeeeha! Cowboy
AJ, aged six,
enjoys a pony ride.

Brian, aged 11,
and Chris
Cawood before
a Little League
baseball game.

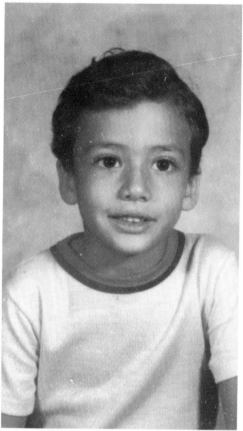

Howie, aged six.

Brian, aged six, with a pudding bowl haircut.

Spikey-haired Nick, aged seven.

Kevin, aged 12, smiles for a special portrait.

Brian, aged seven, and Chris pose with University of Kentucky footballer Bryan Williams.

Brian, aged eight, and Chris dressed up in their Sunday best before singing in church.

Cheeky Brian, aged eight, tucks into a piece of pizza.

Howie, aged nine, dresses smartly for a studio photo

Howie strikes a pose as a budding young baseball player.

Nick, aged 11, the golden boy from Florida.

Nick, aged 12, already looking a singing star on stage.

Brian, aged 15.

Brian, aged 16 at Tates Creek High School.

Brian, aged 17, shortly before leaving school to join the Backstreet Boys.

The cast of Bye Bye Birdie.

Kevin and Dena Riddell, his co-star in
Bye Bye Birdie.

Kevin as Conrad Birdie
in his hit high school
musical, Bye Bye Birdie.

'I was pretty nervous on the first night and had a bit of stage fright, but once I realised how much attention I was getting, I loved it. I remember being able to see my mom from the stage – she was smiling and looking proud. But my main memory was trying to hold up my costume. It kept falling down because it was about two sizes too big. There were about 200 people in the audience and the theatre seemed so big to me. It has been converted into a nightclub since then and I've been back – it's tiny.

'After the first show, I used to pretend to have stage fright because it made all the older girls fuss over me and tell me how cute I was. I convinced people I was scared and said I couldn't go on stage, but inside I loved it. After doing *The Wizard of Oz*, my mum saw I had a big interest in performing and it all went from there. I stopped pretending to have stage fright and just got on with enjoying myself.'

Shortly after that stage debut, Sally Wood, one of Howie's best friends at Fern Creek Elementary School, told him about a new children's theatre which had opened in their area. Sally was a budding young actress and already had a part in the theatre's first production, *Babes in Toyland*. The director, Miss Dani Wood – who was not related to Sally – had finished casting but, luckily, a few weeks before the opening night, a boy dropped out and Howie was brought in. It was the start of a long association with Miss Wood which saw Howie, like AJ, appear in many musical productions and plays. He remained good friends with Sally throughout his school years and they appeared in many shows together.

Howie worked hard at his new-found interest and spent hours learning lines and mastering acting techniques. The children's theatre had an on-going rota of productions and Howie would spend much of his spare time after school preparing his next part, whether at home or at the theatre. He was a disciplined student who grew to love the slog of preparation as much as the fear and excitement of a performance. While most of his school pals were off playing sport, Howie would have his head buried in the script of his next role. His hard work paid off as he gradually won bigger and better roles. When he was 10, he appeared in *The Wizard of Oz* again. This time the Yellow Brick Road had led him from munchkin to the Tin Man, one of the key roles in the show. Sally Wood played Dorothy.

'Acting came very naturally to me,' says Howie. 'I used to enjoy working on my lines and learning music and I did pretty much every show going. I would try to find out through friends and the local newspapers which shows were coming up and where the auditions were. I wanted to do anything to improve my craft. Most kids get involved in sports after school but instead I went to rehearsals and starting having singing and dancing lessons.'

In 1983, around the time when Howie had his triumphant return in *The Wizard of Oz*, two pop acts were dominating the world charts. One was the new all-male American group New Edition, and the other was Michael Jackson, who was making sales history with the album *Thriller*. Both acts caught Howie's imagination. He loved the freshness of New Edition and their big hit 'Mr Telephone Man' and he marvelled at the genius of Jackson. Howie had a wonderfully high voice and was able to imitate Jackson's string of hits which emerged from *Thriller*. Not long after joining Winter Park Junior High School he got his first taste of being a mini pop star when he became lead singer of his first group.

'I was always singing around the house and really got into Michael Jackson. He was so hot at the time and I loved singing songs like 'PYT', 'Billie Jean' and 'Thriller'. When I sang them at school the girls were amazed at my voice. They would say, "Hey you've got an even higher voice than us!" I really got a buzz out of the attention and the more I sang, the more confident I became.

'A few friends of mine already had the basis of a little group. One guy had some drums, another guy from my acting classes had a bass and they knew another boy who played guitar. They were jamming as a group but they needed a singer and they asked me. We were all really keen and performed a couple of gigs. One was at a bowling alley, but things didn't really work out well for us. We wanted to do other gigs, but it became really difficult to co-ordinate everyone to get together because there was always one of us who was busy. It was so frustrating and we didn't last very long. I realised then that it was just too complicated to get a group to stay together.'

Although disillusioned with being in a pop group, Howie was still hooked on becoming an entertainer of some kind. He continued his acting, but his ambitions stepped up a gear when he was 13 and he joined Edgewater High School, near Downtown Orlando. The school offered Howie the facilities and the tuition to develop his skills. Drama classes involved more weighty, demanding productions and the school chorus was run by an enthusiastic director called Laura Shannon, who spotted Howie's talent and was eager to improve his falsetto voice. She loved her choirs to sing *a cappella*, the vocal harmony style which would become the Backstreet Boys' signature. *A cappella* is an Italian phrase which literally means 'as in a chapel' and originated many centuries ago from church choirs which didn't need the backing of musical instruments to sound wonderful. Under the expert guidance of Miss Shannon, Howie began to learn the skill of harmony.

It was an audition Howie went up for shortly after joining Edgewater which he says determined the direction of his life. Up until then he had merely been enjoying the fun of performing, but after winning a role in a production of *Camelot* at a dinner theatre in Orlando, he discovered the potential of earning a living from doing what he loved most.

'I had a tough audition to get the part and was so nervous because I had to cold read from a script they gave me when I got there. The paper was shaking in my hands and I was hoping they couldn't see. It was a straight acting part and was the first time I had to do an English accent. I must have done pretty well though because I got the job.

'I was the only kid in the production and it was very professionally run. I was working with adults who made their living from doing this work, so it opened my eyes to the business side of acting. I had to focus hard because I knew this time it was not just fun and games with some friends. This was business and people were paying serious money to see us.

'I didn't mind being around adults because I was so used to my brother and sisters being so much older than me. Being in *Camelot* made me look at acting in a different light. I was getting paid for the first time and I thought, Wow, this is cool – getting paid for something I enjoyed. I can't remember what I got, but any money for me at that age felt like big money. I didn't have many lines, but I learnt a lot from that show and it was a major step up. It really made me decide to be an actor, or something in the entertainment business. I knew that was how I wanted to earn my living, so my attitude changed and I became more dedicated.'

Howie's hardened resolve to find stardom was soon evident at Edgewater High School. He became one of the most active students in the drama and chorus classes. He went on tours with the chorus, performing in shopping malls and theatres, and even qualified for the All State Chorus, the highest accolade for a high school singer. He also joined the TV production course and learnt how to operate a camera as well as the basics of TV presentation. Pupils at school remember how they often saw Howie working in break times – whether it was singing, learning lines, or catching up on his academic studies. It was remarkable dedication for a teenager and Howie never eased up.

He maintained a jam-packed schedule outside school, too. He continued to be involved in theatre productions and began private singing and dance lessons. Howie also took up an advanced course on acting for the movie camera, which requires somewhat different skills from stage acting. The course paid off when he got the part in a local TV commercial warning children against drugs. The ad led to a job on a cable television show called *Kids Today*, which was followed by a role in a short film called *Seance*. Making a movie sounds glamorous, but Howie admits his debut was nothing to shout about.

'It was a very low budget movie which no one really got to see, but it helped me develop. I was starting to get really serious and I decided entertainment was what I wanted to do with my life. I was doing it all – acting for commercials, taking voice lessons and dance lessons for ballet, jazz, tap. I was in the chorus at school and doing talent competitions, you name it and I was doing it. I wanted to be at the level where I was a well rounded performer in many disciplines, so, whichever one took off first, I would be prepared. I always wanted to have a dual career between acting and singing, but was prepared to go with anything that looked like leading somewhere. There is so much competition in the entertainment business that you can't afford to be weak in any one area.'

Howie's all-round talent soon got him noticed by the army of Florida agents on the lookout for the next movie or singing star of the future. The showbiz scene is notoriously full of chancers making vacuous promises of an easy route to fame. The one main agent Howie signed for did deliver some hope with his contacts in various corners of the industry. But he was the man who wanted Howie to change his name, and so he became Tony Donetti for three years. Howie was uneasy.

'This agent really thought I had something, but he hated my name. He said it didn't stand out or stick in people's memories. He wanted me to have a more catchy name and he came up with Tony Donetti.

'I wasn't really happy about changing my name, but I just went with it. I felt awkward because I wondered if people would ever get to know me, if I ever got popular. I thought they would only know Tony Donetti, not Howie Dorough, and I didn't like the thought of that.

'I wanted my family to be recognised and for my mom to be proud and be able to say that's her son up there. I hated having a stage name and I also didn't like being marketed as something that I wasn't, just because the agent thought I looked Italian.

'The agent took me to New York and got me signed up with three of the big agencies. I did a lot of auditions for commercials and sitcoms, but there was a writers' strike at the time, so I didn't get too much work.'

Despite the rejections, Howie managed to get some professional work during this period. He appeared in the children's TV series *Welcome Freshman* and was an extra in two movies, *Cop and a Half* and *Parenthood*, a hit comedy starring Steve Martin, in which Howie is visible in a classroom scene. It was an exciting break and a step in the right direction.

Howie also gained some minor ground in his pursuit of pop stardom by appearing in a duet with a girl from school. They performed various chart cover versions in a number of talent contests and Howie got his first taste of fame, albeit on a tiny local level. He says: 'Our duets got a good reception and some of the younger girls in the audience were attracted to me. After the shows they would ask me for my autograph. I liked it and thought, Wow, they look at me as if I am really a somebody. They were always saying, "One day, Howard, you're going to make it – just keep on going." Things like that gave me a lift when I was finding it tough to make a big breakthrough.'

While Howie was lapping up his small slice of adulation, he couldn't help but marvel at Bobby Brown's successful solo career, which took off in 1988 with the singles 'Don't Be Cruel' and his big hit, 'My Prerogative', a song Howie particularly liked and began to use in auditions.

Bobby Brown had been in New Edition, which was created by music producer Maurice Starr. Starr had lost control of the group just as they hit the big time, but he had spent several years since developing a new all-male teen band, which was already taking off. They were the New Kids on the Block.

'I always used to dream about performing in front of thousands of people. I idolised Bobby Brown and when the New Kids came along they really hit me. All my young nieces were into them, so I saw all the videos and got to know the songs. I looked at that band and thought, I would *love* to be part of something like that.

'At one stage I learnt all the words to their big hits and tried to get into the group. My mom saw Maurice Starr on TV one day and made a note of his name. I found out the address of the fan club and made a tape of me singing New Kids songs and a couple by Bobby Brown. If one of the New Kids quit, I thought I could be there waiting to replace him. I was so desperate to be the sixth New Kid that I sent the tape off, but I didn't get any response.

'My mom said to me around that time that I should put a group together of my own, but I had seen how hard it was to organise a band in school, so I said, No, that's too tough, I'll just go solo.'

Even though Howie was struggling to make a genuine impact in the professional entertainment world, he was still something of a celebrity at school. Along with Sally Wood, he was one of the key drama students and was also the undisputed star of the choir. So it came as no real surprise when he was asked to sing the national anthem in a ceremony before a big basketball match.

Howie was flattered to be asked and felt it was a simple enough job which was well within his capabilities. There would be around 400 people in the audience, which was no problem because he was comfortable singing in front of crowds. He had sung the anthem every school day since he was five, just like all American kids, so what could possibly go wrong? How mistaken he was. Howie cringes when he recalls what happened.

'My choir teacher asked me to sing the anthem because the last few people had got so nervous they forgot the words. She thought I would be perfect because I was so used to singing and acting, but she still suggested I write the words down, just in case. I said, "No problem, I won't need that, I know the song so well." She said, "Are you sure?" I was so confident, I insisted it would be easy.

'Everyone in the school thought I would do a good job because they knew me from drama and the chorus. Even the basketball coach came up to me and said, "Hey, Howie, we're so glad you're doing the anthem for us. It was really sad when the other guys messed it up, but you'll do a great job." I said, "Yeah, thanks, I'm happy to do it for you."

'The gymnasium was full, but I was still relaxed. I picked up the microphone and suddenly I saw all my friends and the cheerleaders and my mind went totally blank. I was singing a cappella but I hit the first note way too low – it was like a bass part when I was a tenor. Hitting the wrong note totally freaked me out. I tried harmonising my way up to the tenor part but, by concentrating on the music, I suddenly realised I was singing the wrong words.

'I could hear myself saying the lines and I was thinking, Heck, what did I just say? I looked at the faces in the audience and I knew I was messing it up. I could see they were thinking, Oh, no, he's goofed up like the others. I then skipped a line and got some more words wrong. Finally, I got it right and finished it well, but, by them, the damage was done.

'I was so embarrassed it wasn't even funny. When I finished, the cheerleaders came over and said, "Hey it's OK, Howie, don't worry," but they were all laughing behind my back. I felt so bad. Everyone was looking up at me to sing well and do them proud, so I felt I had let everyone down. I couldn't believe I didn't remember the words to my national anthem, but I guess the pressure got to me. I felt terrible and once the game started I said to a friend, "Quick, let's get out of here."'

Thankfully, Howie laid the ghost of his basketball day disaster to rest before he left Edgewater High. The opportunity came during the autumn term of his last year when he sang a solo number at a talent contest in front of the whole school. It proved to be his greatest and most memorable performance at the school and it still lingers in many former pupils' memories.

At the time, the movie *Ghost*, starring Patrick Swayze and Demi Moore, was a box office smash and the film's theme song, the Righteous Brothers' 'Unchained Melody', was catapulted from the archives to number one worldwide. Howie's brother Johnny suggested he should try singing it and, after weeks of practising at home to an instrumental backing tape, Howie had it perfected. He unveiled the song in front of more than 800 pupils and all his teachers in the school auditorium. There were no prizes at stake in the talent contest because it was more of an entertainment showcase, but Howie stole all the honours for a sensational performance.

He stood on stage in a smart waistcoat and black trousers and had the audience mesmerized by his immaculate rendition of that moving song. Girls had tears in their eyes and boys looked on in envy. Howie was note perfect and, this time, he was word perfect too. His national anthem mess was forgotten as the screams filled the auditorium and everyone jumped to their feet.

Pam Meizlik, who did drama with Howie, will never forget that performance. 'All the girls fell in love with Howie that day. He sang the song so beautifully most of us were crying. When you closed your eyes it sounded like the record – it was that good. It was so romantic, everyone wanted to be his girl.'

Certainly, the experience had a major effect on Howie and he remembers it well.

'It was the first time I had really done anything like that as a soloist. I was so nervous before going on stage because I wasn't sure how people would react, or if I could pull it off. The response was amazing. I brought them to their feet and the girls were screaming. It was the first time that had ever happened to me and it felt fantastic.

'Loads of people congratulated me afterwards and even my chorus teacher was amazed I could sing like that. From then on she always got me to sing to groups of 12-year-olds who visited the school to have a look round before they joined. I sang 'Unchained Melody' for them. They wanted my autograph and I was even asked to sing at end of year graduation parties. A few months after doing that song, I had built up my own little fan club of young girls – some even wrote to me at my house.

'At the time, I had a girlfriend who was a year behind me at school and I was still going out with her after I graduated. Whenever I went back to pick her up, so many of the girls remembered me for that song and still asked for my autograph.

'Singing 'Unchained Melody' was a turning point for me. I

saw the vision that I could maybe do something in that field. I had dreamed about being Bobby Brown or in the New Kids and suddenly I had a real small taste of it.'

Howie capped his dramatic efforts at school by being jointly named the Most Talented Actor with Sally Wood. He passed all his exams and went to study for an arts degree at the university in Tampa, a city on the west coast. He could have gone to a college in another state, but stayed in Florida because that was where he stood the best chance of getting a showbiz break.

He continued attending auditions under the name Tony Donetti during his first year at university and came close to joining a popular Spanish group called Menudo, but that fell through after his second recall because his Spanish was not quite good enough. As a solid future in the entertainment world looked more and more unlikely, Howie started thinking about an alternative career. He had been trying for so many years to get that big chance, but he couldn't wait forever, so he planned to become a show business lawyer should his dreams come to nothing. At least he would be working on the fringe of the business he loved, and it would certainly provide a good living.

But, just after finishing his first year at UCF, he got the call from Gloria Sicoli and his legal plans were dismissed, as he recalls.

'I had just gone on vacation to Puerto Rico when Gloria called. When I got back, my dad told me about her call. I spoke to her and she said they had already seen some boys, but I could still have an audition. I thought, What the heck, go for it, so I went over to Lou's house not expecting much. I had no idea who he was or what he did.

'There was a video camera there and I thought he was some kind of casting director. I sang a couple of New Kids songs and then 'Unchained Melody' and 'My Prerogative'. After the audition, they said AJ had been in earlier and they liked him, so I told them I knew him pretty well. They asked me if I was interested in joining a group once they found some more guys and I said, Sure. It sounded really positive, but I didn't hear another thing after that. I gave up on the whole idea and figured either it had collapsed or they had found someone else. I forgot about it and got on with some other things.'

What Howie didn't realise was that he *was* in the new group. Lou and Gloria had loved his audition and thought he was perfect. But, a few weeks later, Gloria had to stop scouting to begin some other work, so she handed over her files to a theatrical manager called Jean Tanzy, who had been representing AJ. In the melee of the handover, Howie's contact numbers, photo and details were lost. Suddenly Lou Pearlman had no way of contacting the talented singer he wanted for his band. Lou says: 'It was so frustrating. We had found one of the guys we wanted, but we had no numbers for him. We were going through the phone book looking for a guy called Tony Donetti, but we had no idea he didn't exist.'

4

TEARS OF A CHILD STAR

It would take a coincidence and a fair slice of luck before Howie came back into Lou's path to claim his rightful place in the Backstreet Boys. The immediate worry facing Lou, however, was maintaining the momentum after Gloria's sudden departure. She had got the project moving and had spread the word about the group among the young hopefuls of Florida. Gloria was due to return to help Lou and Jean Tanzy, but sadly, soon after finishing her other work, she was hit by a serious muscle-wasting disease which left her unable to work. It was impossible for her to continue and it would take an agonising two year battle before she recovered. Lou has always credited her with helping him get the Backstreet Boys started and, years later, when she was finally well enough to travel, the boys would honour her invaluable contribution at a glittering ceremony in Germany.

Lou looked to Jean and her partner Sybil Galler to continue the talent search. After years in entertainment management, both women had extensive experience at the grass roots level of the business, so they were well capable of spotting the boys needed for a New Kids-style group. More adverts were placed in the *Florida Blue Sheet* and for the next couple of months Jean and Sybil sifted through hundreds of applications, as well as the boys left unseen on Gloria's files. They then staged auditions for the hundred or so who made the shortlist. The boys had to perform New Kids songs and a choice of their own and a short dance routine choreographed by AJ.

Instead of using Lou's house, Jean and Sybil set up the video camera, a sound system and a small stage in a warehouse in Kissimmee used to store spare parts for Lou's giant airships. With airship frames, fins and nose caps littered all around, it was certainly an odd location to test out young performers, but it had a certain irony. When assembled by an expert engineer, those cumbersome lumps of machinery could be made into a graceful and awesome flying machine which can soar to great heights and grab the attention of millions. That is precisely what Lou was trying to do with the motley assortment of boys at the warehouse. He was the inventor and engineer with a blueprint to piece them together and create a glorious musical unit at which fans worldwide would marvel. Lou had turned airships, which were considered outdated wartime white elephants, into skyway billboards and money-making machines. He knew he could revolutionize the lives of five young ordinary boys in much the same way. He already had two critical parts for his invention in AJ and the elusive Tony, and now he needed the rest.

The star quality of the first boy to audition in the warehouse shone through. He was only a small lad of 12, but he had the personality and all-round ability of someone bigger and older. As a bonus, he also had angelic blond looks. His name was Nick Carter and Lou knew immediately he was perfect for the group.

'As soon as I saw Nick perform, I knew he was just what we needed. He was a cute kid with a great personality and he was really professional for his age. When he sang, he had control of the microphone and had a great voice. You could tell he was already a well-seasoned performer, even though he was just a kid. Jean and Sybil were impressed with him too.

'I spoke to his mum afterwards and told her that I was almost certain we would want Nick, but we still had to look at the other guys. She was really sweet and said she was worried about Nick's education should he join the group. She also said he had been offered a job with the Mickey Mouse Club on television. I said I couldn't promise to be like the Walt Disney company, but I assured her that I was giving this group my very best efforts. I promised her that Nick would be well looked after and would get all the right tutoring. I said I would do whatever it takes to keep the boys happy. Right then I started to wonder what I was letting myself in for. Starting a young group sounds great, but I began to realise there were many other responsibilities that came with it.'

As much as Lou and the others liked Nick, he wasn't actually among the first choices. After seeing the rest of the auditions, they initially selected another boy, but he changed his mind about the group a week later and quit. Lou, Jean and Sybil looked at Nick's video footage again and asked him to join.

After his warehouse audition, Nick had talked excitedly to his mum throughout the four-hour drive to their home in Tampa. He loved the idea of being in a teen pop group and he could tell Lou was seriously committed to the venture. It emerged later that Nick had met AJ and Howie at various auditions and had all got on well, which is how the three became the core of the Backstreet Boys.

As Nick pondered the prospect of joining the group, his big dilemma was what to do about the Mickey Mouse Club job. That too was a great opportunity and, on the surface, was a better bet than a pop group which probably wouldn't lead anywhere. The TV show would guarantee him plenty of work and exposure and its producers were promising a lengthy contract, a valuable commodity for any aspiring young performer. It seemed crazy to Nick that he had been trying to get a break for several years, only to face rejections, yet now he had two chances right at the same time. When the first choice boy quit, Lou offered Nick the job. Now he had to choose.

He talked it through with his mum and dad, who both then had long chats with Lou to clear up any worries about Nick's education. Finally, they were happy with his promises and so was Nick. He took the big gamble on possible pop stardom in the future, instead of instant TV fame. In the long run, it was the best decision of his young life. It was also the right move in the short term because, a few months later, the Mickey Mouse Club was scrapped and all its cast were back on the demoralising audition circuit.

Nick's childhood, in any normal definition, effectively ended when he joined the group. His life would now revolved around the tight unit of the band, private tutors and working solidly to achieve success. But he had enjoyed a busy and colourful childhood up until then. Nicholas Gene Carter was born on 28 January 1980 in a tiny suburb of Western New York state called Jamestown. He was the first child for his mum, Jane, although his dad, Bob, also had a daughter from a previous marriage.

Jamestown is a small community and Bob owned a restaurant in the town. It had a small dance floor and doubled up as a mini disco at night. Occasionally, he let the disco be used for junior nights and it was at one of these events that young Nick first showed signs of being a budding little performer. His parents remember him as a toddler dancing confidently, and with some rhythm, on the dance floor alongside the older children. Virtually all youngsters get up and dance at some stage, but Nick's parents noticed that their son loved it just that little bit more and would snap up any opportunity to dance when he was in the restaurant.

When Nick was four, the family moved to Florida and eventually settled in Ruskin by Tampa Bay, a few miles south of the city. Bob and Jane began running a retirement home there for old people. Florida was a wonderful change from New York and young Nick loved it as much as his parents did. Not only was the climate so much kinder, with mild winters and hot summers, but the general lifestyle seemed so much more favourable for raising a family. Soon after settling in Ruskin, Jane had twins, Aaron and Angel.

Nick's first school was Miles Elementary and it was there that his singing and acting talents were discovered in a small production of the musical *Phantom of the Opera*. He was seven at the time and remembers it well.

'I wanted to be involved in the play when the teachers first started talking about it, but I missed out. Luckily, the guy who was playing the police inspector Raoul chickened out after a few rehearsals, so I stepped up and asked the teacher if I could do it. She asked me to sing for her. I hadn't really done that much singing before, so I was pretty shaky, but she liked my voice and I got the part.

'It was only a fun school play with a small set and props made by the teachers and some of the parents. It was nothing fancy because we were just little kids, but it was my first ever play, so it was really exciting for me. The audience was very responsive to my bits and it spurred me on. It made me think I was capable of performing and gave me a lot of confidence to do other things.'

Nick was instantly infected by the performing bug and, in the next five years, he worked continuously to improve his all-round entertaining skills. Gradually he started to see that maybe there was a future for him in some area of show business. Nick's mum responded well to his interest and, like Denise McLean, supported her son every step of the way. Jane arranged for Nick to have singing lessons with Marianne Prinkey, a teacher who would play a crucial part in his early development. She taught him singing techniques and how to get the best out of his voice, as well as the rudiments of stage performance and how to use a microphone professionally.

Marianne's business partner was Sandy Karl, and both women were closely involved with coaching the Swashbucklers, a dancing and cheerleader group which performed on match days for the Tampa Bay Buccaneers American football team. It was rare to have a young boy who was so keen to be an entertainer, so Marianne and Sandy took Nick along to rehearsals and built him into the act.

An angelic looking blond boy was a perfect contrast to the lines of pretty girls in the Swashbucklers and soon Nick became the front man for part of the pre-match and half-time shows. He would sing in front of a 55,000 crowd with the Swashbuckler girls dancing behind him. Nick was only 10 at the time and it was a mighty step up from singing in front of parents or school friends, but he loved the adrenalin that flowed from the attention. 'I got such an amazing buzz when I went out on the field,' he says. 'I couldn't believe I was singing in front of so many people. One of my proudest moments was when I had to sing the national anthem before a game. There was so much pressure on me, but it was an incredible feeling to hear the cheers when I finished.' Thankfully, Nick didn't suffer the memory loss which had struck Howie before the school basketball game.

Nick's confidence swelled with his success in the Swashbucklers and he became more involved in other performing ventures. He entered several talent shows and chalked up his first victory with a cool Elvis Presley impersonation singing 'Hound Dog'. He joined a dance troupe which travelled around Florida competing in big shows and also recorded a demo tape with a producer called Mark Dye at a studio in St Petersburg. The first tracks Nick ever recorded were songs by his favourite band, Journey, an American group he still loves today.

Nick wanted to get more involved in the professional side of the business, so he started going for TV and film auditions. His mum drove him around, but it wasn't easy to find the time because she had two elder children – Lesley and BJ – as well as the twins to look after. But her help was rewarded when Nick got his first part in a film. The good news was that he had the leading role; the bad news was that it was in an art house project called *Elektra* which was destined for a tiny audience. Whatever the limited impact of the movie, it was still good for a budding child star to get any sort of film work.

Nick's next break in movies was the flip side to his first. He was signed to appear in the major Hollywood production *Edward Scissorhands*, which starred Johnny Depp and was directed by Tim Burton, the man who brought Batman to the big screen. The down side to being in such a big movie was that Nick's so-called 'part' was reduced to nothing more than a background blur by the time the film was released.

'It would be going too far to say I was actually *in Edward Scissorhands* because I was so far in the background that you can't tell it's me. It would be better to say I was on the set of the film. A lot of kids in Orlando get small parts in films. I was in the scene when Edward looks out of a window to the neighbourhood. For a split second he sees some kids playing – one of them was me.

'I was sliding on a yellow piece of plastic we used to call a Slip n' Slide. They were long flat sheets with water coming out of holes and were really popular with kids at the time. I had to slide on one in the background of a shot. It was great fun being on the set, but it was really cold and they made us do it a lot of times. I didn't get to speak to Johnny Depp but he was there and we were all watching him. I walked into the wardrobe room and saw the map of his outfit which was pretty interesting.

'I went for a lot of auditions around this time, but I was not that good at acting. I was very inexperienced and the competition was really tough. I managed to get in a pilot for a TV show but that never came to anything. My heart wasn't really in acting because I loved singing above everything.'

Unfortunately, as Nick enjoyed the fun of his mini showbiz career, his modest success cast a dark shadow over his school life. He had been happy at Miles Elementary, but things weren't so friendly when he graduated to Orange Grove and then Young Junior High Schools. Both schools were in rougher parts of town and his child star pretensions brought a hostile reaction from his classmates.

Many boys were jealous of Nick's achievements, no matter how small they were in real terms, and they resented it when he was let out of lessons early for auditions. At first, Nick was the butt of verbal jibes about his singing and acting and for being 'girly' because he didn't play sports. To compound his problems, Nick was small for his age, which made him a soft target, so the teasing escalated into outright bullying and physical intimidation. Nick began to dread every day at those two schools and the tears of fear and unhappiness flowed.

He was hurt, scared and confused by his experiences, particularly at Young Junior High where he spent his last year of formal schooling before leaving to have private tutors full time. It wasn't only the bullying from boys which was upsetting, but also the treatment Nick got from girls. Pretty girls shunned him because he wasn't part of the gang and those rejections would shape Nick's attitude to relationships years later when he had thousands of girls at his feet as the main heart throb of the Backstreet Boys.

'I will never forget the treatment I got at those two schools. I would not classify myself as a nerd, but I was not into sports because I was always singing and acting. Some guys held a grudge because I did that and they always gave me attitude. They were always wanting to start fights with me for no reason at all. If you looked at someone the wrong way, or they thought it was the wrong way, they would want a fight. I wasn't the type who liked fighting and I always walked away. But it was dangerous to turn your back because those guys didn't care – they came after you anyway.

'I was real small back then – half the size I am now – so I got picked on all the time. They hated me for getting time off school and, in their eyes, I wasn't one of them.

'I really wish I could have enjoyed school but I hated it. I had no real friends because I was offset from everybody else. I used to dread going to school and got upset a lot. I don't know if it was because I was afraid of getting into a fight, or I was afraid of school in general. I think it was so unfair for the kids to treat me like that. I never did anything to make people angry, or show off about my singing. I was just doing the thing I loved. They went against me from the start and there was nothing I could do to stop it.

'The girls were just as bad and they didn't like me either. It was like, Who is he? Just because I wasn't popular or like the guys who did sports, they didn't want to know me. They saw the cool guys being tough on me, so they thought they had to do the same.

'When I was a kid, I dreamed of having a pretty girlfriend and I had a crush on a few girls, but they only wanted to hang out with the cool guys, not me. I found that the girls who were kind to me back then were not necessarily the pretty ones, but they were good on the inside.

'Since I've been in the Backstreet Boys, I am always asked in interviews, "What is your dream girl?" I tell the press that my ideal girl is not some pin-up gorgeous model. I look for a girl who has a good heart first, before I care about how they look. I don't say that because it's nice and diplomatic, but because I experienced the reaction from both types of girls when I was a kid and I know which is more important.

'It was girls with good hearts who had time for me when it mattered, whereas the pretty ones didn't care. Because of what happened to me, I strongly believe you should never judge people by how they look. The only thing that matters is what's on the inside.'

Luckily for Nick, his junior high school misery ended when he got the job in the new group. From then on, Nick had private tutors and didn't have to suffer any more taunts from bullies. The Mr Bigs of the playground probably cheered his departure and claimed some twisted victory, while the pretty girls by their side giggled stupidly in awe.

Within a few years, Nick's life would have changed beyond recognition and the tables would have turned dramatically. Who knows what happened to those bullies, who cares, because Nick would be a tall, handsome young man with millions applauding his singing talent, not ridiculing it. Those sad days at school would be fading memories as he enjoyed an amazing life as the fair prince of a far bigger playground. Thousands of girls, many of them very pretty, would be shunning the attentions of cool guys at school to dream of being Nick Carter's girl.

5

BAND HOUSE HARMONIES

The most rewarding moment of the warehouse auditions came near the end of a long day when a familiar face walked through the door. Lou beamed when he saw him and called out excitedly: 'Hey, Tony, where've you been? We've been looking for you everywhere.'

Howie was very flattered, if a little bemused by the reception.

'I wasn't sure what was going on at first. It had been a few months since I'd been to Lou's house and I had given up the whole idea of his group. I hadn't heard a word, so I assumed it had been scrapped or they had found all the guys they needed.

'Then I had got a call from one of my agents who asked if I wanted to audition for a new pop group. I said, "You know, this sounds very familiar. I think I have already done this." But then I thought, why not, I'll go up for it.

'I was so late for the audition, I nearly didn't make it. The first person I saw was Lou. Then AJ came over and said, "Hey, man, you don't have to do this audition, you're already in."

'They were really pleased to see me and were joking around that I was the missing person they had been searching for, but had been looking for Tony Donetti. When Lou said he wanted me for the group I knew I couldn't pass it up. I so nearly didn't go to that audition, but I guess fate took me there.'

The name Tony Donetti had been created to bring Howie fame, but it nearly cost him the biggest break of his life. As Howie reflected on the near miss and focused on the future, it seemed the perfect time to leave his pseudonym in the void of obscurity and let his true identity take centre stage.

There were two other guys selected from the warehouse auditions to make up the magic five. They were Sam Licata, who knew Howie from college in Tampa, and another Orlando boy called Charles Edwards. Sadly, they were destined not to last the distance.

Now five talented boys had finally been found, the real work had to begin. Their varying natural talents had to be fine tuned so they worked as a slick, professional group. They needed voice training, choreography, songs to sing, styling, publicity. You name it and a group of raw youngsters need it to succeed in the pop world. The list was long and very expensive, but it all had to be done if they were to stand a chance of getting the all-important item at the top of the list – a record deal.

Jean and Sybil controlled the day-to-day running of the group, while Lou took care of the business side and bankrolled whatever they needed. He paid the food bills, gave the boys pocket money and paid for tutors. Lou got Bob Fischetti, his good friend and right-hand man in the aviation business, to keep track of all the bills. And there would be many. Lou also drew up a formal business structure, so that everyone owned a certain number of shares in the group.

During the first few weeks the boys rehearsed at the warehouse and at a dance studio, but the problems were soon obvious. They mostly lived in different areas of Kissimmee and Orlando, but the real worries were Nick and Sam. They both lived in Tampa and it was ridiculous to expect them to commute and still be fresh for a hard day's work. Sam was 19 and could handle it, but Nick was only 12, so a solution had to be found.

Lou had promised he would give the project his full personal and financial support and he quickly proved this by renting a two-bedroom house in Kissimmee which became known as the Band House. It was near to AJ and Charles' homes and Howie was driving, so it was no problem for him to get there. Sam moved into the house while Nick and his mum stayed there for several days at a time to ease the burden of travelling.

Everything revolved around the Band House. It was the office, the vocal training centre, even the school and the motel. The garage was converted into a dance studio: a special wooden floor was laid on the concrete to protect the boys from developing shin splints and full length mirrors were drilled to the walls. In the early days, AJ taught the boys dance steps, but later a professional choreographer was brought in.

The bulk of the work was on singing and harmonising the boys' voices. At the time they couldn't play instruments, so the principal aim was to create a technically faultless vocal harmony group. Mastering the *a cappella* style would give them an identity and respect within the music business, as well as fans. The house was nearly always filled with singing and they would often spend hours practising just one song until they had it right. They had no material of their own, but they were all big fans of successful American harmony groups such as Boyz II Men and Shai, so they used their songs. They also practised some New Kids songs, which would give them a faster section when it came to doing their first shows.

Apart from endless rehearsals, one of the first things a new group needs is a name. There have been many wrong versions of how the Backstreet Boys came up with their name, but this is how it happened. It was a tradition in the early days to regularly meet Lou for dinner to discuss how everything was going and to kick around new ideas which would help the group progress. One of their favourite venues was TGI Friday's on International Drive and this is where they created the name. Lou remembers the evening well.

'We came up with loads of names that night, but we didn't like any of them. We were sitting in a booth by a window and I looked out. Across the street was a flea market called Backstreet Market where a lot of the local kids used to hang out. AJ, Nick and Howie used to go there sometimes. At the entrance was a big sign for Backstreet Market. I said to the guys, "What about Backstreet?"'

'We all thought about it for a while and said the word a few times. Everyone liked the sound of it. Then we started trying to think of another word to go with it and we all more or less said "Boys" at the same time. It had a certain flow and ring to it which we all liked. The word "Boys" was a natural choice because we were always saying, "Where are the boys going today, what can the boys do next?"

'Right after we came up with the name I started drawing it in big letters on a notepad. I always carried a pad around to keep track of any ideas we came up with. The exact way I wrote the name for the first time that night was the Backstreet Boys logo we still use today. The flea market has since been built over to make a shopping mall, but I guess its name still lives on.'

The first few months were a slog. The boys worked for hours on end each day perfecting their harmonies and dance routines. There were many tense moments, particularly when fatigue set in, but they were all committed to the group, so any disputes or personality clashes were quickly forgotten. Jean and Sybil kept them to a strict schedule and when the pop star training stopped, the younger guys had private academic lessons. Nick and AJ had yet to graduate from high school, and Howie continued the second year of his arts degree by studying at Valencia Community College in Orlando.

The group's act developed quickly and soon they had several *a cappella* songs mastered, as well as some New Kids tracks which they sang to a backing tape. The time drew near for them to test their voices outside the Band House. Jean brought in one of her contacts, Scott Hoekstra, an enthusiastic agent with good connections in the local entertainment market. Once he heard them sing he was happy to try and get them some gigs. 'I was really impressed,' he says. 'I liked Lou and I believed in the boys. I knew how to get them noticed, so I devoted all my time to getting them bookings and some exposure. I was really excited about the whole idea.'

Pretty quickly, Scott got them their first gig in Fashion Square Mall, one of Orlando's biggest shopping centres. They performed a couple of *a cappella* tunes and their New Kids songs to a backing tape. It was not the most glamorous venue, but it was a start. This debut was followed by a slot on a cable television show and

46

appearances at business conventions, including a short gig in front of 1,000 film industry executives at Disney World. They then appeared at a nightclub called Pleasure Island and around Christmas time they sang at a restaurant called Celebrities. Although they were far from famous yet, Lou made sure they were treated like stars. They were taken everywhere in his limousine or one of the Rolls Royces, so that an illusion of fame was created which would generate hype. The gigs were for a few hundred people at most, but the boys were willing to sing anywhere to get their name known, and they always arrived and left in style.

By the start of 1993 the fledgling group already had many local appearances under their belts, thanks to Scott. The experience had helped sharpen up their singing and Lou was convinced it was worth spending the money to get them into a recording studio. Scott knew a talented producer called Tim Coons who was happy to help prepare a demo tape. Unfortunately, that's when the rot set in.

The first song the boys recorded was 'Get Ready', which had been a hit for The Temptations back in 1969. The next was 'Loverboy', a song written by Lou's close friend in New York, Bob Curiano, who did some early Backstreet Boys producing. Then they did 'Save the World', which Sam had written, and 'Tell Me That I'm Dreaming', which Lou had written with a little help from Howie. The recording session seemed to go well, but a little while later two serious problems emerged.

Firstly, Tim was not happy with Charles' voice on tape. Secondly, Sam suddenly decided he didn't want his song used to promote the group. In the following weeks both matters festered and finally came to a head.

Finally, it was mutually agreed they should both leave.

It was a nightmare scenario for Lou.

'We had only been going a few months and already there were problems. Tim told me that Charles' voice wasn't recording right for the sound we needed. There was nothing we could do except tell Charles he had to go. It was all above board and all the guys and I went out for dinner to talk about it with him. There was no rash decision. He understood where we were coming from and accepted that we had to try someone else. He was really upset because he loved being in the group and we didn't like losing him, but those are the sort of decisions you have to make. It wasn't to be, but I told him that if he got anything else together I would help him.

'Around the same time Charles left, the problem with Sam's song came up. I was completely taken aback when he said we couldn't use it. We had spent thousands of dollars recording the song, but suddenly he wanted to keep it for himself. We couldn't just forget about it. I said to him, "You've got to be a team player in this, or it's not going to work."

'Everyone was finding it hard in those early months. We were starting from nothing and were trying to find a direction. It didn't make things any easier when we had problems like that. We all had to help each other, but it was clear that Sam was more focused on a solo career and Sybil was behind him. That was no good for the Backstreet Boys and there was some friction over the whole matter. It was disappointing but, in the end, it was decided he should leave. It was very much a mutual decision.'

Lou compensated Sam, Sybil and Charles for their input to avoid any legal wrangling in the future. He kept his promise to Charles and supported him in a new group, but he quit that one to get married.

Sam and Sybil began a relationship a few months after leaving the Backstreet Boys. They now live in Nashville, Tennessee, and plan to get married. Sam has recently signed a solo recording contract and is bringing out a country music album. He has no regrets about his decision to leave the Backstreet Boys, despite their success. He says: 'Leaving the group was one of the hardest decisions of my life. I loved those guys and I loved Lou. I respected what they were doing, but my heart was not in the musical direction they were heading. I was worried about not being able to shake off the stigma of being in a boy group way off in the future. I had seen that happen to singers like Donny Osmond and I didn't want to take that risk.

'I knew the Backstreet Boys could make it because of Lou's

incredible commitment. I remember he said to me one day that he was going to make it work, even if it meant losing everything, and I believed him. His determination was amazing and with him behind them I couldn't see how they could fail. I'm pleased they're doing well. They deserve it.'

Losing two members was hardly ideal, but the core of the group was AJ, Howie and Nick and they were as committed as ever. In a way, it was better to find out sooner that things weren't quite right, rather than later. After all, there was no point putting a beautiful airship in flight if it didn't have the right amount of helium to keep it in the sky.

Any truly capable entrepreneur can generally turn a negative into a positive and Lou did just that when Sam and Charles left. Two employees in his company had independently told him about a talented young man who was working at Disney World. He had dark, brooding looks and could sing and dance well. Without hesitation, Lou put out the word to get this guy in for an audition. His name was Kevin Richardson.

6

AN ARENA IN THE HILLS

Kevin Richardson's path to the Backstreet Boys had been a harder and more circuitous journey than the route taken by AJ, Howie and Nick. He was not a Florida boy and was never part of the Orlando child acting scene. Kevin was from the mid-eastern state of Kentucky some 800 miles north of the Disney World rides. Not only is Kentucky a long way geographically, but it's also a world away from Florida in character. Florida is a fast-moving commercial state, with sprawling cities, wonderful beaches, extreme wealth and an international economy supported by tourism. In contrast, Kentucky has few big cities and is principally a rural state with small farming towns amid vast areas of open fields and mountains. It is famous for its world class horse breeding trade, with the Kentucky Derby as its showpiece event, and a lucrative tobacco industry. But, as most locals will testify, nothing much happens in Kentucky, which is why Kevin Richardson packed his bags when he was 19 and went in search of fame in Florida.

Kevin had a happy childhood in Kentucky and always talks fondly of his years there. He was born on 3 October 1972 in Lexington, the second largest city after the state capital Louisville. When he was three, his dad Jerald and mum Ann wanted to get away from city life, so they took Kevin and his two older brothers, Jerald Junior and Tim, to live on a farm just outside Harrodsburg, a small town 40 miles to the south-west of Lexington. It wasn't a working farm, but it had 10 acres of land, a horse, two ponies, some chickens and a cow, so the Richardsons were able to lead a self-sufficient country life. At times it may have been a solitary world, but it was one full of adventure for Kevin and his brothers. Kevin in particular grew to love the outdoor life; he spent long days exploring the countryside and became a good horse rider, helped by Jerald Junior, who trained horses and competed in the state fair. Having two older brothers was tough for Kevin because they would tease him, beat him at sport and always win fiercely contested wrestling matches. He would end up bruised and upset, but competing with them made him strong and he quickly shone out in Little League baseball and football.

The Richardsons were a tight-knit family with a household run by strict discipline. Kevin's dad was a physically strong, imposing figure, and he expected his sons to stick to the rules. They all had chores around the farm which had to be done along with their school homework, or they would be punished. Jerald may have been strict, but he was also a fair man with strong principles, and Kevin always respected and loved him. He loved his mum, too, who provided a gentler balance to his father's discipline. 'I owe everything to my parents,' says Kevin today. 'I was very lucky to be brought up with all the love and support any child could ask for. My father was firm with us boys, but he taught us to be strong and to always work hard. My parents gave me everything I needed when I was growing up. They encouraged me in all the things I wanted to do and I give them all the credit for anything I have achieved.'

Singing was one of the first activities Jerald and Ann encouraged young Kevin to pursue and it began with the church choir. Both parents were committed Christians, so all the boys were brought up to follow a strict faith. Jerald and Ann were actively involved in the choir, too, and were often asked to sing solos. Some of Kevin's earliest memories are of travelling to church on Sunday mornings with his family singing in the car all the way there and all the way back. The music continued at the farm where the latest songs blared out from the radio or his brothers' record players. Kevin says: 'Music and singing were always part of my life, right from when I was a little boy. All my family loved singing and it always made me happy. I joined the church choir and then the choir at elementary school.

'One of my favourite classes was music. When I was seven, the music teacher played a pop song on the piano and asked the class to sing along, but I was the only one who knew the words. I can't remember what the song was, but I must have heard it on the radio and picked up the words. The teacher asked me to sing to everyone and all the kids were looking at me. It was the first time I ever got attention for singing and I remember thinking, Hey, I like this.'

It came as no real surprise to Jerald and Ann that Kevin had a natural talent for singing because there was a long history of music in the family. A host of distant relatives on Ann's side played piano by ear or sang well, and her father sang in a barbershop quartet, an all-male harmonising group know for singing romantic songs, popular in America in the 1920s and '30s. But Kevin's natural flair and ambition for music wouldn't really emerge until he was nine and the family had moved to an even more remote home.

Cathedral Domain was Kevin's home for the next nine years and his experiences there had a lasting impact on his life. The Domain is a church-owned youth camp, secluded in woods 300 feet up in the foothills of the Appalachian mountain range, which borders Kentucky to the south. It was founded in 1946 by the Bishop of Lexington, William Moody, who had a dream to create a haven in the countryside where city folk could relax and worship. In the following years the camp was slowly built on the hillside at the end of a narrow mountain road by its first manager, Glenn Adkins. He oversaw the construction amid the woodland of large log cabins, dining rooms, a recreation hall, a swimming pool, kitchens and, finally, a big church. School children from eight to 18 years old came there for summer holidays with a mixture of religious studies and outdoor activities. It still runs successfully today and, in winter when the trees are stripped of foliage, the giant red cross of St George on the front of the church can be seen from Highway 52 below.

Jerald Richardson took up the post of manager of the youth camp after hearing about the vacancy from his sister. Cathedral Domain is 60 miles south-east of Lexington, and lies between two towns, Beattyville, 10 miles to the south, and Irvine, 12 miles to the north. It would be an isolating, but enriching existence for all the family. The first accommodation was a log cabin, but Jerald set about building a house for the family on the hillside next to the church. It took a year to build and Kevin and his brothers helped with the labour. They all grew to enjoy the solitude of winter on the hill, as much as the buzz of activity when the camp was full in the summer with more than 200 holidaying youngsters.

There was an old, slightly out of tune, upright piano in the big recreation hall and it drew Kevin like a magnet. He had played around briefly on a church organ before, but he'd never had a piano at his disposal. He eagerly let his fingers find their way across the keys during those first weeks at Cathedral Domain. To his astonishment, he could play by ear just like his ancestors.

'I clunked away at that piano and found I could pick out notes from songs I'd heard on the radio. I was pretty amazed I could do it, but I knew about my relatives, so I guessed it was in my blood. The first song I learnt to play was 'Don't Stop Believing' by Journey. I was a big Journey fan and they were my favourite band at the time. A buddy, who was older than me, played it for me first and I watched and learned how to play it. I thought he was really cool because he could play the piano.

'From then on I played the piano whenever I could. I had a lot of time to fill living there, so it was a perfect place to learn. I spent hours on my own just letting my fingers feel their way across the keys. I would hear a song and pretty soon I could play it.'

Cathedral Domain is in Lee County, but, luckily for Kevin and his brother Tim, it is only a short distance from the border line with Estill County, which gave them an option to go to school in either area. It was fortunate because both boys were mad keen American football players and only the Estill County schools in Irvine ran good teams, so Kevin enrolled at junior high and Tim went to the high school there. It marked the beginning of a double life for Kevin, with one set of friends at school and a separate life and social circle at Cathedral Domain.

Each day Ann or Jerald had to drive the boys to Irvine and collect them in the afternoon. It is a tiny rural town, lying over an iron bridge on the banks of the Kentucky River. The centre is just a few streets of old buildings, shops and the local newspaper office. Highway 89 from Lexington runs straight through the town but it only takes a few minutes to drive through. A railway for freight trains carrying mainly tobacco and coal runs parallel to the river. Irvine is a place where everyone knows each other and a new face in town is noticed almost immediately. Despite the closeness of the people who have lived in Irvine all their lives, the Richardsons were welcomed warmly and soon became a well liked and respected family. They would travel into town each Sunday for service at the River Drive Christian Church by the railway terminal.

Kevin was a popular pupil at junior high and made friends quickly. He was big for his age and established himself as one of the best players in the football team. He liked Irvine, but when the summer arrived he also discovered the true wonders of living at Cathedral Domain. Not only was the countryside beautiful, but the camp was transformed into a hubbub of activity as it filled with boys and girls of all ages on holiday from all over America. Kevin had a ready-made bunch of friends to explore the hills with and play sport. He remembers it fondly: 'It could get real lonely up there in the winter, but the summers were fantastic. I made so many great friends from all over the US. It was confusing at first because I got attached to people, but after a week they would go home. I found it weird emotionally and would cry when I had to say goodbye. I wouldn't see them for a year, or sometimes never again. It took a while for me to get used to making friends, having a ball all week, then watch them leave. The good thing was that a whole other bunch would arrive and I would be happy again. I had an incredible childhood because I had two lives and two sets of friends. I was really lucky.'

One friend he made at the camp was Keith McGuffey, who was from Danville, a two-hour drive away. They shared many interests, especially a love of music. Keith could play piano by ear, too, so they would try and copy their favourite pop songs on the old piano. The two boys became like brothers and when Keith returned each summer he was treated like a fourth son in the Richardson household. He is still Kevin's best friend and was one of the key security men for the Backstreet Boys, as well as the rapper Trey D on the European music scene.

Kevin, aged 18, in his senior year at high school.

AJ, aged 14, at Denn John Middle school.

AJ, aged 15, at Osceola High School.

Howie, aged 14, in glasses during his first year at High School.

Howie, aged 15, in his High School year book photo.

Howie, in his mortar board and gown for the Honour Society.

Howie, aged 18, in a tuxedo for a school dance.

Surrounded by girls, Kevin in the school drama class.

Howie in his drama class.

Kevin on the
touchline watching a
football game.

The house Jerald Richardson and his sons built at Cathedral Domain.

The recreation hall at Cathedral Domain where Kevin performed the first song he wrote.

Two-tone AJ, aged 13, was always a bit wacky when he was a kid.

Kevin, aged 15, poses in his football strip.

Howie and classmates singing for a school ceremony.

Looking cool in a waistcoat, Howie poses with the chorus.

Howie sings in the Edgewater High School chorus.

Howie won the Most Talented award with childhood friend Sally Wood.

Howie was always studying or rehearsing lines during break times at school.

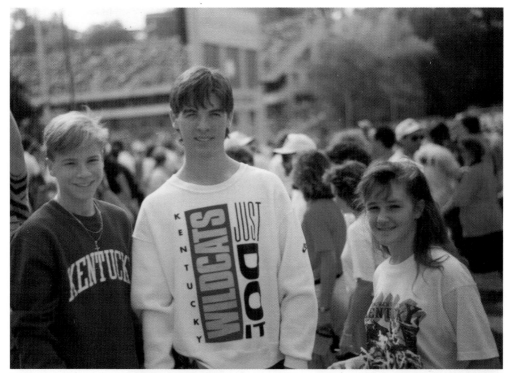

Even as teenagers,
Brian and Chris
were inseparable.

Muddy and exhausted,
Kevin lines up after
a hard match.

Howie in his days as Tony Donetti.

Brian, aged 18.

Smooth AJ, aged 16, poses for a
professional shot.

One of Kevin's modelling photos shortly
before joining the Backstreet Boys.

At Cathedral Domain Kevin and Keith were paid to be team leaders. They had a list of duties, including cleaning the cabins and the pool, mowing the grass and sweeping the volleyball court, but their main responsibility was making sure the younger groups had a great holiday. In the mornings, the two boys would take Bible reading lessons, then organise long hikes and picnics and sports activities throughout the afternoons. In the evenings, they arranged entertainment for all the camp. One of their favourite events was Skit Night, when campers were invited to perform in front of everybody in the recreation hall. They could do a short acting sketch, tell some jokes or sing. Anything was allowed, as long as it was entertaining. Soon Kevin and Keith became the stars of their own Skit Nights.

It all started when Kevin was 13 and got a synthesiser for Christmas. It was a perfect present because he was getting bored with the old piano and wanted an instrument to imitate the heavy rock bands of the early 1980s which were using synthesisers. One of his favourite groups at the time was Van Halen, whose single 'Jump' had been a huge hit, and the first sequence Kevin taught himself on his new toy was the famous introduction to that song. It was an exciting moment because suddenly he was playing the sound of real pop stars.

Kevin played that synthesiser for hours on end in his room during the long winter at the empty camp and, by the time Keith returned the following summer, he was already a skilled player. It was great to have his buddy back and this was when they wrote their first song together.

'We were in one of the cabins one day and we just started writing a song. I was on the keyboard, tapping the keys, singing some words and Keith was writing it down. Every now and then he would say, "Yeah, that's good." One of our favourite songs was 'When Love Comes Walking In' by Van Halen, so we took that chord structure and modified it.

'After about 30 minutes we'd finished our song. It was called 'As Time Goes By'. The lyrics were pretty cheesy when I think of it now, but I still remember the words. The first verse was: *If I were with you, You were with me, Together we could make it eventually, Because I am the one, The one you need, Our lives will grow stronger, And soon you'll see.* Then the chorus was: *As time goes by, And days have past, You're the only girl, And the others come last.* As I said, it's really cheesy!

'There was a Skit Night at the camp soon after we wrote that song and that was the first time we played it to anyone. There were about 30 people there – I was on the keyboard and Keith was singing with me. I was a little hesitant at first because, although I liked to sing, I didn't know if my voice was pleasant to hear. But the feedback was fantastic and they all wanted to have a copy of the song. I loved singing it for everyone and after that night people started giving me positive reinforcement about singing and writing songs. My mum and dad couldn't stop talking about it and whenever anyone came over they'd say, "Come on, Kevin, play that song you wrote."

'That song was definitely a pivotal moment in terms of my ambitions to be a singer. It was like, Yeah, I've got a voice people like. My confidence developed and I thought I had something worth pursuing.

'Keith and I got really excited about our song. He had a friend who had a home studio, so I stayed at Keith's for a week and we recorded a tape of the song. I've still got the tape and I've listened to it a few times since then. There I am, 13 years old, singing my first song. It sounds pretty funny.

'After that, Keith and I wrote songs whenever we got together and we used to talk about having our own company one day which we would call K&K Productions. We still want to do it. We completed 20 songs back in those days and we had about 30 unfinished. I would come up with music by just feeling with my fingers and listening. I found writing lyrics harder, so Keith did that. Lyrics are tough because you have to think about what you are writing and I'm so critical, I analyse the words too much. I quit halfway through because I think it's garbage instead of finishing and making changes later.

'I loved the whole idea of being a pop star when I was a teenager. I would pick up a hair brush and pretend it was a microphone and sing along to the radio. When the camp was quiet and there was just my family around, I would sing outside real loud. I would sing to the grass and dumb stuff like that.

56

'There was an area of the camp where you can look down over a big valley – it was like a bowl. I used to go up there with a broomstick and pretend it was like a concert arena. I would stand on the hill and sing at the top of my voice. It seemed pretty good because it echoed. I felt like I was on stage up there and I would sing all kinds of songs by Bon Jovi, Michael Jackson and Prince. It sounds kinda crazy when you think back, but that's what I used to do.'

After joining Estill County High School Kevin's other life away from the camp became busier. He was there for four years and quickly became involved in various school activities. He was a dedicated student, who worked hard at all subjects and got good grades. He was also the only boy to be in both the choir and the football team. His brother Tim was already a respected player in the senior team and was nicknamed Tom Cat. It wasn't long before the football players nicknamed Kevin, Kittie Cat.

It was a rare combination for a boy to be a good singer and a talented sportsman, but Kevin could do it all. Many of the girls in the choir remember having frequently to wait to start rehearsals because Kevin was playing football. He would dash in late, full of apologies, his hair still wet from the shower, but they didn't mind because many of them had crushes on him.

One of Kevin's closest friends throughout high school was Shawn Jones. They played football together and hung out in a foursome with their first steady girlfriends. Kevin's sweetheart was Christi Ore, who was best friends with Shawn's girlfriend, Melissa Lewis. Christi was 16, a year older than Kevin, when they started dating. The two couples went to school dances together after football games, traditionally the big social event for teenagers in Irvine. They also went on long hikes from Cathedral Domain, or simply watched videos at one of their homes. It was Kevin's first relationship and it lasted nearly three years. Christi, now married with children, recalls it.

'Our first date was the Valentine's Day dance at school. Kevin gave me a rose that night and was really sweet.

'We were both young while we were dating but we had a lot

57

of fun. Kevin was a real funny guy and I liked being with him. Because I was a year older I was the one who drove us everywhere in the early days. There wasn't a lot to do in Irvine so we would normally just cruise around and hang out. We were real close and at the time it felt like we were in a serious relationship, but we were just teenage sweethearts.

'Kevin loved singing and sang to me all the time. I played the piano, too, but I could read music. Kevin could only play by ear, so I tried to teach him, but he couldn't pick it up. It made him so mad he couldn't do it.'

Whatever Kevin's technical shortcomings, his playing was improving dramatically. He had such confidence on the keyboards that he entered a talent contest at school early in his second year and performed 'As Time Goes By' and a Van Halen instrumental in front of 1,000 pupils. It was a far more discerning audience than the young campers at Cathedral Domain and he didn't have Keith with him for support. But Kevin took his keyboards into school and Christi looked on proudly when he sang perfectly and got a standing ovation.

That was the first of many school talent contests for Kevin. Because so few people wanted to take part, he found himself doing up to three or four different pieces. As his fame grew within the school, it prompted some resentment from other boys.

'There were some guys who gave me a hard time, but I didn't let it bother me. They would call me "pretty boy" and stuff like that. The guys in the football team gave me support and that was all that mattered. It was pretty rare for a guy to be in the football team and to sing too.

'The talent shows had to last at least an hour to be worth having, but very few kids had the guts to do something in front of the school. I was involved every year and the teachers always asked me to do more bits. I would end up doing several different things because so few people took part.

'One year, I did some *a cappella* duets with another guy and some short drama scenes and once I did a comedy sketch which I had seen on television. It involved a comedian impersonating all the players in a football team as they introduced themselves before a match. They were all crazy characters. I had done the sketch for the guys in my team once and they loved it. They said, "You've got to do that at the talent contest for us."

'I was scared of doing it in front of the school because I wasn't sure people would find it funny. Before I started I said, "You guys might not find this funny, but I'm doing this for my buddies in the football team." But the reaction I got was amazing – everyone in that audience was rolling in the aisles laughing. I'll never forget the buzz I got. When I sang the girls loved it but you could see guys weren't interested – some of them hated it. But with that comedy sketch, I had them all laughing and it was a fantastic feeling to be able to do that.'

Spurred on by his talent contest successes, Kevin threw his energies into trying to kick start a music career. He devoted more time to the school chorus and was selected for the All State Choir, and also formed an amateur rock band with some school friends; but that was frustrating. They spent many hours rehearsing cover songs, but it was soon obvious the others didn't have the same degree of dedication as Kevin. Various drummers and guitarists came and went without the group ever progressing to a level where they could perform a gig.

Kevin also recorded some more songs with Keith at the studio in Danville, but the hopes of getting a record deal from a basic demo tape were, at best, remote. As his high school days passed, Kevin started to fear that his technical weaknesses on the keyboard would stop him from pursuing a professional career. Why would anyone employ a musician who couldn't read music?

Nor was the future bright for Kevin's relationship with Christi. It had hit problems when she left Irvine to go to college. They broke up once, only to get back together a few months later, but eventually drifted apart. Christi says: 'We never really said it was over, it just fizzled out. We remained good friends and there were no hard feelings because we had a great time. We were so young when we started dating that it couldn't be expected to last forever.'

Kevin's next steady girlfriend was a blonde cheerleader called Kristy Flynn. Although she was two years younger, it developed into a serious and more adult relationship. They became the golden couple of the school. He was the dark, good-looking footballer and entertainer and she was the classic, pretty all-American girl.

As Kevin began his final year at high school, he was under increasing pressure from his teachers and parents to decide what he was going to do with his future. His chances in music were limited, so it was either work or go to college. Finally, Kevin took a radical decision and decided to live out his other boyhood dream – to be a fighter pilot – so he enlisted in the airforce. It was quite different from pop stardom but, for him, it was the next best thing.

He says: 'I had to come up with a positive direction because it looked like music was not leading anywhere. I only had natural talent. I was really frustrated because music was all I wanted to do. I didn't want to go to college, so I joined the airforce. It seemed like the right thing to do. I had always loved the idea of being a pilot after seeing the movie *Top Gun* and I had flown in some small aircraft before. My grandfather worked at Lexington airport and had taken me up a few times and I'd had a couple of flying lessons. I felt that the airforce would be a worthwhile career and I'd be able to earn a good living.'

Kevin was not due to join the ranks of airmen until he had graduated at the end of the school year. Soon after signing up, his mix of talents won him the lead role in the high school's first ever musical, *Bye Bye, Birdie*. The story centred around Conrad Birdie, a 1960s rock star in the mould of Elvis Presley, and his No.1 fan, a small-town girl who seeks one last kiss from her idol before he joins the army. Kevin was rarely involved in drama but was considered the only boy in the school fit for the part because he could sing well, looked great and had musical ambitions of his own.

The storyline certainly seemed ironic considering Kevin's underlying pop star dream and his recent choice of career. He relished the role and it gave him his biggest early taste of fame. *Bye Bye, Birdie* was a major event in Irvine and is still remembered by many people. The show played to packed audiences over four performances and was seen by the whole school, as well as virtually everyone in the town. It raised Kevin to minor celebrity status in Irvine.

Kevin's girlfriend was in the show, but the lead female role went to

Dena Riddell who played the besotted young girl, Kim. She remembers what an impact he made.

'That role was made for Kevin. There was really no other boy in the school who could have played it. He was quite a heart throb and I remember lots of girls saying how much they liked him. Even back then he could make a girl faint. He had something special and I always thought he would shoot off from Irvine as soon as he got the chance and make something of himself.

'We rehearsed the show for eight weeks and everything revolved around Kevin. He would come running in from football practice and rehearse in his sweat pants. But we didn't mind waiting for him because he was so charming. He was the kind of guy who doesn't want to let anyone down.

'The whole show was so exciting and I was the one who got to sing with Kevin on stage and kiss him. Kristy was a good friend of mine and she and Kevin were the perfect couple in school. They were really in love. Kristy got to be with him in real life, but I got to be his girl on stage. It was all so much fun and everyone loved the show. People still remember that one more than any others they've done since.'

Kevin dreamed of being someone like Conrad Birdie in real life, but sadly the reality could not have been more different. Once he had taken off his gold satin jacket and the hair spray had been washed out to flatten his extravagant quiff, he was back to being Irvine wannabe Kevin Richardson, with stars in his eyes and no real hope of a music career.

The high of the *Bye Bye, Birdie* triumph was soon overshadowed by galling disappointment on the football field. Kevin's team had enjoyed one of the best runs in the history of the school and were through to the semi-final play-offs against Lincoln County. Nearly 4,000 people turned out to watch the game at the high school and it looked like Estill County were going to win. They were in the lead, but in the closing minutes Lincoln scored to win 15–12. Kevin slumped to the ground in tears. His coach, Hoover Niece, did all he could to console him. He remembers: 'Kevin played his heart out that day and we were so close to winning. There was so much expectation riding on the game. He took losing so hard and was sobbing at the end. A lot of the other guys were crying, too. I had a real close team and we laughed and cried together. I told Kevin that he would always be a winner because when he did something, he always gave it everything he had. We had parties at Cathedral Domain after some big games and Kevin would always get up and sing for us. He was the life and soul of the party normally. We went up there after that game but the atmosphere was really sombre and no-one was in the mood. He didn't sing for us that night.'

Kevin graduated from high school in 1989 and spent the summer working in a fast food restaurant and on tobacco farms, as well as helping at Cathedral Domain, while waiting for his enlistment date. He was resigned to becoming a pilot when, out of the blue, he got a phone call which would ground his flying dream.

The call was from the man who ran the small studio in Danville where Kevin had recorded some songs with Keith. A musician working there was looking for a male singer for a new group and the technician wondered if Kevin was interested. It seemed like a great opportunity, so Kevin drove over for an audition. The musician already had two women singers in their thirties and was looking for a fourth member. Kevin was a bit too young, but the man liked his voice and offered him the job. The plan was to develop a middle of the road act which would perform popular cover versions at lounge bars, high school dances and community halls. The musician was certain the money would flow in.

The set up wasn't exactly perfect for Kevin. It was a long way from home and the others were a lot older, but to get paid for what he loved most was better than serving burgers and humping tobacco in the baking fields. He took the job, delayed his start date for the airforce, and moved to Danville. Kevin says: 'I decided to give it a shot because I thought I would earn some good money before I went in the airforce. We rehearsed for a while then played at a couple of parties, some clubs and a high school dance – it was all pretty low profile stuff but it was going OK.

'I asked to delay my recruitment a little longer, but this time my recruiter said No. I said, "Why won't you let me delay it a couple more months? You did not recruit me, I came to you, you did not have to work to get me." I told him that I wanted to see how the band worked out, but he said, "Either you join now or not at all." So I said No. Something inside me was saying I should stick with music.'

The group was called Paradise, but unfortunately it proved to be a living hell in the long run. After six months' hard work they were still performing at third rate venues and Kevin would often drive several hours for a gig and hardly cover his petrol costs. Thankfully, he was earning good money as a sales rep for a lawn care company in Lexington so he could support his failing music career, but he was disillusioned and depressed. He had thrown away an exciting career in the airforce for lofty dreams of pop stardom, but his fantasies had crashed and burned. He had blown it. Paradise was not going to succeed and Kevin wondered if he would ever get the break he needed. After all his efforts and all the songs he had written, he was still a nobody in a small town. He craved excitement and glamour and it was clear he wouldn't find it in the slow, rural wilds of Kentucky. He had enjoyed his upbringing there, but now he wanted different things from life. He had out-grown the area he loved. His relationship with Kristy was over, the band wasn't working out and he hated his job. What was keeping him there? It was then that Kevin decided the only option was to leave for good.

He was working at the lawn care company with his best friend from school, a guy called Jimmy. Over lunch one day, Kevin made one of the biggest decisions of his life.

'I was only 18 and was making good money in that job, but I wasn't happy. I wanted to make something of myself and I didn't feel it was going to happen in Kentucky.

'My mom and dad had just been on a cruise to the Bahamas and they had talked to a bunch of the entertainers. They were really young people and they reminded my mom of me. When she got home she said, "Honey, you should go to Florida and audition for one of those cruise ships. That would be a great job for you – do something that's fun."

'My dad said, "Son, you're young, you have nothing holding

you down. I'm not trying to get rid of you because you're already out of the house, but if I was you, I would move somewhere, do something different. You can always come back here if it doesn't work out. Just go and see what happens."

'This really stayed in my mind and one lunch break I said to Jimmy, "We got to get out of this town. Why don't we just take off and go to Florida?" He loved the idea and we got real excited.

'At first, we were going to wait until the end of the month to pick up our next pay cheque so we would have more money. But, by the end of lunch, we'd decided to leave the next day. We quit our jobs and that night we packed our clothes and told our families we were going. The next morning we got into Jimmy's car and drove to Florida. It was so exciting and it was the best thing I ever did.'

The moment Kevin and Jimmy arrived in the bright May beauty of Florida, they knew they had made the right decision. They headed for Orlando, the Mecca for holidaymakers from around the world, and Kevin could feel the fun and energy and was filled with optimism. If he was going to make it anywhere, surely it was here. They both got jobs at Disney World easily. Jimmy took a post in the car parking section and Kevin became a tour guide. He was disappointed he had missed the auditions for the entertainment jobs, but he loved being a guide because he was dealing with happy people on holiday, which was a million times better than attending weed-riddled lawns in Lexington.

His parents came down for a holiday and were joined by Jerald Junior who was working as a model in Miami. They all proudly took Kevin's Disney tour. Ann and Jerald had a fantastic time in Florida and were thrilled their son's gamble was paying off. It was good to see him so happy and revitalised by the change. As they headed back to Kentucky, Ann and Jerald were happy in the knowledge that their youngest boy was enjoying life again. It was a weight off their mind. At last, everything was working out for all their sons. Tragically, the happiness of the Richardson family would soon be devastated.

Not long after returning from Florida, Jerald fell ill. It started with stomach pains, which he ignored for some time, but they gradually worsened. It was unlike Jerald ever to acknowledge he was ill. He was such a strong man, who always shunned pain and soldiered on, not wanting to cause anyone any bother. This time, however, even he could not ignore the stabbing discomfort. At first Jerald feared he had an ulcer, so he went for an examination at Lexington Hospital. The truth was far more serious: he had cancer.

Jerald and Ann decided not to tell Kevin right away. There was nothing he could do and they didn't want to worry him unnecessarily. The doctors felt confident the tumour was operable, so Jerald had an emergency operation. It appeared to have been a success and, following a course of chemotherapy, it looked like Jerald could beat the cancer. He slowly regained his strength through the winter at Cathedral Domain, but as the summer approached, the cancer returned. This time, even Jerald's power and determination could not win.

Kevin was told about the seriousness of his father's condition and flew back to Kentucky. It was a devastating shock to see how much the disease had weakened his dad. His weight had plummeted and he no longer had the strength to go outside. Finally, Jerald had to be moved from the beauty of Cathedral Domain to a hospital bed where he battled for another forty days. Jerald died on Monday, 26 August 1991. Watching the agony of those final days, seeing his strong, proud father slowly fade away, ripped through Kevin's world and changed something inside him forever.

'When I first found out my dad was sick, I thought he was going to be OK. He was a big, strong man, I didn't think anything could hurt him. He was such a solid rock and if he was ever sick he never complained about pain.

'After the chemotherapy, it looked like he was going to beat it, but all of a sudden he got really bad and I moved home. When they finally told me he was going to die, I couldn't believe it. It made me grow up very quickly and changed me.

'He was on his death bed in the hospital for 40 days. I would go and see him and stay with him, but we never really talked about him dying. When I look back now I wish we had, so I could know what he was thinking.

'Once my mum left the room and it was just me and my eldest brother there. Dad said, "Take care of your ma for me." He didn't say anything else about him dying, just for us to look after mum.

'The first time I realised he knew he was going to die was when he said to me, "Well, I guess I'm not going to get to see my grandbabies." When I heard that come from his lips, it just ripped me apart.'

The entire Richardson family was devastated by Jerald's death, as were so many people who had known and respected him throughout his life. Cathedral Domain, so full of fun and youth in the summers, was a sad place that year. There was a service at the church on the hill and the funeral was held in Lexington.

Kevin was heartbroken and shattered, but, apart from the deep grief, there was also anger and confusion. His father was a good man, who lived with integrity and faith in God, so Kevin couldn't understand why his life had been so brutally cut short. How could he be taken when he had been so selfless and giving? In the months that followed, the pain continued to torture Kevin's heart and mind.

If there was one positive outcome from all that pain, it was how it changed Kevin's perspective on life. His father's death made him aware how quickly and indiscriminately life can be snuffed out and made him determined to seize every opportunity as if it were his last. This awakening hardened his resolve to make something of his life and inspired the drive he needed to make it with the Backstreet Boys.

For the immediate future, Kevin realised he had to leave Kentucky again.

'I stayed in Kentucky for many months after my father died to be with my mum and my brothers, so we could support each other. I was working in a warehouse and delivering office supplies and furniture. I was very depressed and knew I had to get away. It was the winter and it was cold and raining.

'I knew there was nothing for me in Lexington and felt there was something calling me back to Orlando. I don't know what it was, I just felt I should go back. I didn't see my future in Kentucky and, when I felt I was emotionally strong enough to be on my own again, I left.

'Losing my father affected my outlook on life. It hardened me emotionally, but it made me stronger and I feel, having gone through that, I can cope with anything. It made me realise that life is short and you can go at any time and you have to take every opportunity you get. It hit home to me that if you want anything out of life, you cannot just sit around and wait. You have to go and make things happen.

'My father instilled strong values in all of us. He taught us to work hard and I know that as long as my body is physically working, I am not going to starve. As long as I can work I will always survive, whether it is in entertainment or working in a restaurant. His philosophy on life was to live it to the full, which is why he encouraged me to go to Florida.

'Losing him motivated me and made me more determined. And when I got back to Orlando, it almost felt like he was still alive.'

Kevin's new-found drive was soon apparent as he steadily stepped up his work load over the next year. He continued at Disney and transferred to the entertainment section where he appeared in a stunt sequence as one of the Ninja Turtles, as well as Aladdin in the character parade. He joined a local theatre group and landed a job in a dinner theatre show. As if this wasn't enough, Kevin had some professional photographs taken and started modelling and also became a dance teacher. It was this volume of activity which, indirectly, led to his chance with the Backstreet Boys in March 1993.

Kevin's girlfriend at the time had a flatmate, whose boyfriend, Bob Dunham, worked for Lou Pearlman. Bob knew about Kevin's pop star dreams and he also knew that Lou was still trying to fill the new group. Bob told Lou about Kevin. Around the same time, Kevin met Lisa Fischetti while he was working at a convention. Lisa is the wife of Bob Fischetti, Lou's right hand man for twelve years, and the person entrusted with keeping track of the cost of the pop venture. Lisa gave Lou Kevin's modelling card.

Lou brought Kevin in for an audition and liked what he heard. He also took him to the recording studio to make sure the producers were happy. They were and Kevin became the fourth Backstreet Boy. He says: 'I was very excited when I was told I had the job. Everything seemed to fall into place. I was taken down to the Band House to meet the other guys. When I heard them sing, I was knocked out. I thought, Wow, this is the shot I've been waiting for.'

7

WILDCAT CHOIR BOY

It was great news to have Kevin in the group. He settled in easily and began rehearsing with AJ, Howie and Nick at the band house. But they were still missing that all-important fifth member and it was becoming a more pressing problem. Jean Tanzy had auditioned several more boys, but none was suitable and Lou was anxious for the group to progress and begin doing more live performances. The bills were mounting up, yet he was still no nearer to having a settled group, let alone a record deal. Scott Hoekstra was still working hard and had lined up promotional work around Orlando which would raise the Backstreet Boys' profile, but there was little point doing gigs with a fragmented band.

Kevin had suggested they audition his cousin, Brian Littrell, who he had grown up with in Lexington. The two boys had sung frequently in church together and Kevin knew Brian had a beautiful voice. He also knew that Brian was a hard-working and good-looking 18-year-old who would fit in well. At first, Lou wasn't keen on the idea. He wanted to find a local kid and did not want the added complication of bringing a schoolboy down from Kentucky – it could be riddled with problems – so they continued to scout in Orlando.

After several more fruitless weeks, Lou finally said, 'Okay, Kevin, you better give your cousin a call.'

Monday, 19 April. Brian Littrell was in an American history class at Tates Creek High School when he got the call that would change his life. A voice came over the Tannoy system: *Urgent telephone call for Brian Littrell. Please come to the office immediately.*

To a youngster, a call during lesson time is like the phone ringing in the middle of the night for an adult: it strikes a gut-wrenching fear inside that tells you it can only be bad news. That's exactly what happened to Brian. It was two o'clock and he was in the last lesson of the day. He would be home in half an hour, so what was so urgent it couldn't wait until then? He tried to look calm in front of his classmates and walked as casually as he could from the back row to the door. But beneath the exterior his stomach was turning and his mind was flashing through the worst scenarios. Had there been an accident? Was someone in his family hurt?

Out in the corridor, his bravado vanished. He broke into a gentle trot and then into a darting run as his panic escalated. He nervously picked up the phone and his fears turned to confusion when a vaguely familiar voice cheerfully asked, 'Hey, cous', What's up? How ya doin'? It's Kevin.' Brian remembers that conversation vividly.

'I couldn't work out what was going on. My mind was in a panic because I thought something serious had happened to someone in my family. It was a relief to hear a happy voice, but I was confused. I hadn't really heard much from Kevin since he went to Florida, so he was about the last person I would expect to call, especially to get me out of class. I said: "What's going on, Kevin, why call now?"

'He said, "I've met these guys and we're starting a band. We've been looking for another member and I've told them about you. They want you to come down to Florida so they can meet you. How does that sound?"

'I hadn't heard anything about this before, so I was really shocked. I was saying things like, "Is this really true, Kevin? What's going on?" I thought he must be serious, otherwise he wouldn't call from Florida. I couldn't stay on the phone there, so I asked him to ring me at home at 3 p.m. I got back to class and told my friend, Rob, about the call. I said, "That was cousin Kevin. He wants me to join a *pop group*!" Rob looked at me and said, "Wow. That sounds cool!" The whole thing was really weird.'

Brian got into his yellow and orange Nissan pick-up truck, nicknamed the Bleedin' Banana by his pals, and raced home. He sat anxiously by the phone and began to worry when the clock ominously ticked past three o'clock. Maybe the whole thing was a wicked joke, he thought. And then Kevin called and told him what had happened in the past few weeks.

Brian listened intently to the story about the man with the millions and the boys who sang soulful *a cappella* and, slowly, he realised that the offer of pop stardom was no joke.

'When Kevin didn't call dead on three, I started sweating and thinking, He's not going to call, this isn't for real. But when he called and gave me all the details, I realised this was the opportunity of a lifetime.

'It all happened so fast after that. I called my mum at work and she already knew all about it. It turned out Kevin had spoken to her first to make sure it was OK to call me. He knew that if my parents were against it, there would be no point getting me all excited.

'When my parents got home we talked about it really seriously. The first consideration was my school work because I had another year left before I graduated. My mind was going crazy and I was talking real fast. I couldn't stop thinking about the possibilities.

'At 9 p.m. Kevin called from Lou's house. Lou had a chat with my parents and told them about his commitment to the band and assured them that I would have tutors so I would still graduate. I then spoke to Lou. He was very informal about everything and didn't want to push me. I was in the kitchen and he wanted to hear my voice, so I sang the chorus of the Luther Vandross song, 'Here and Now'. He said I sounded good and wanted me to come down.

'I didn't know if I had the courage to go through with joining the group. I was scared and didn't know what I was getting myself into. I knew I had a good singing voice, but I had never really wanted to be in a pop band, or even thought about earning a living in the entertainment business. I thought I may use my singing to help me get a scholarship to college, but nothing beyond that. This was a whole new thing for me and I felt like I was jumping in head first. But I knew I had to go for it, so I said Yes.'

Brian got the 6 a.m. flight from Lexington to Orlando the following morning. His mother explained to the school principal why he wouldn't be there for a few days. Flying out of Lexington was no problem – it is a small airport – but Brian got a shock when he landed at Atlanta to get a connecting flight. It is one of the world's largest airports and Brian felt intimidated. He may have been 18 years old, but he had never travelled on his own. He got the monorail to the main terminal with no problem, but got out to find himself in a giant terminal with thousands of people dashing around. Loneliness and the enormity of what lay ahead began to descend on him.

He had one incredible stroke of luck which lifted his spirits. He stopped two men in flight uniforms to ask directions to his next departure zone. He showed them his ticket and, amazingly, they were the pilot and co-pilot of his Orlando flight, so he followed them right to the gate. It struck him as a good omen, but as he waited to board the fear started to hit him again. Once he boarded the plane, he knew there would be no turning back. He felt scared and longed for the security of Lexington, so he called home.

'My folks weren't in, but my brother was there,' says Brian. 'I don't know what got into me, but as soon as I heard his voice I started crying my eyes out. I guess it was a mixture of fear and being homesick. The airport was really intimidating and I didn't know what I was getting involved in. It had all happened in such a whirl. I thought, What am I doing here? I should be at school in class with my pals. My brother gave me one of those big brotherly support chats. He boosted me up and said I had to go for it, and that I could do the audition, no problem. He told me not to worry and that if it didn't work out, then I could come home and everything would be back to normal. He made me feel a bit better, but I was still real scared.'

It was no real surprise Brian feared his jaunt into the unknown. He had always lived in the same small area of south Lexington since his birth on February 20, 1975, and had led a relatively closeted life with an extremely close family. It was a bond which emanated from when Brian was five and he became so gravely ill that doctors were certain he would die.

The traumatic period began with an innocuous accident such as every young child suffers. One afternoon Brian was happily riding a scooter following his mum, Jackie, on her bike near their home in Winnipeg Way. He hit the curb, flipped over and grazed his knee. There was some bleeding and plenty of tears, but, after a good hug, Brian was playing again and the cuts began to heal under some Band Aids. Two weeks later, Brian and his brother Harold, who is three years older, were playing in the street outside their grandfather's house. Harold was riding his bike at top speed when Brian slipped in his path. He couldn't steer away and accidentally ran clean over his brother's stomach.

Brian screamed in agony and his mum and dad, also Harold, came running over. There was no obvious sign of injury, but he had hit his head badly and they were worried he might have fractured his skull. They took him to hospital and were relived when X-rays showed no fractures, but other tests revealed some shattering news: Brian had a tiny hole in his heart and was suffering from a rare and life-threatening blood infection.

The defect in the bottom of his heart had been with Brian all his life but was not serious. The infection, however, which originated from the first accident, had spread dramatically through his bloodstream and doctors feared it would kill him. Brian explains: 'The infection was so bad that the doctors had no way of getting it under control. My parents were told that it was a very rare condition and few people ever survived. Because I was so little, the chances were even worse. The doctors basically gave me a zero per cent chance of living.

'I didn't really know what was going on because I was so young. One minute I had been running around having fun, the next I was in hospital having all kinds of treatment. I was terrified.'

It was the beginning of a period which would test the faith of Harold and Jackie Littrell. They had been deeply religious people all their lives and followed a strict Baptist faith, but their belief in God was stretched to the limit as they watched their son's condition worsen during two months in hospital. Brian himself remembers the fear.

'It was awful being in hospital for all that time. I had to lie very still and had so many drips in my arms that they had to start using the veins in my feet. The doctors would literally beat my chest to break up the infection. I had to be held down and I would cry and scream. I didn't know what was going on, but I felt I was going to die in that hospital.

'My mom was by my side every day and night. Whenever I woke up, she was there. She prayed all the time I would get well, but nothing was happening and I was getting worse. She felt that God was taking her baby away prematurely, but she didn't know why it was. She was holding on to me so tightly, mentally and physically.

'My mum told me later that she started praying differently after she spoke to my dad's mom. She had told her that I belonged to God and I was only on loan. She also said that if God wanted to take me, she'd have to let me go.

'My mom couldn't bear to let her baby die, but she started to pray that if that had to happen, then all she asked was I be taken now and not have to suffer any more pain. She thanked God for my life, even though I was only five years old. It was so hard for her to say those prayers, but she made herself let me go.

'It was incredible, but from that point on I slowly started to get better. No one expected me to pull through – the doctors were amazed. Everyone thought I was going to die, but it all changed after my mom started praying differently. I honestly believe it was a miracle that I survived.

'The whole experience affected me dramatically as I got older. I was really close to dying, so I appreciated everything that bit more. I feel blessed to have had such a wonderful life since then.

'When I first got out of hospital, I was still very weak and couldn't do the things kids normally do, which was pretty confusing. I had been cooped up in a hospital and I wanted to have some fun, but I was told to take it easy. The infection had gone, but I still had the hole in my heart and everyone was worried about that.

'There was a soccer coaching course going on behind my house just after I got out of hospital and I wanted to join in. My parents wouldn't let me. I didn't understand what was going on and I had to watch the other kids playing soccer while I kicked a ball around on my own. Then I discovered basketball. My parents weren't so worried about that game because it was not so physical. I used to play it all the time because it was just about the first thing I was allowed to do after getting better.

'I had to keep having tests on my heart, but I started to lead a normal life again.'

Brian missed so much of school while he was ill that he had to be held back a year at Landsdowne Elementary. He felt uncomfortable being the oldest in the class, especially as he was one of the smallest. The good news was that he met Chris Cawood in that new year and they became best friends and inseparable. They would sit together in all classes, hang out together at break times and spend nearly every hour together after school and at weekends. They were both sport fanatics and would fill all their free time playing football, soccer, baseball and their favourite game, basketball. Brian's PE teacher at elementary school, Larry Donithan recalls: 'Brian and Chris were like a pair of bookends. If you saw one, you would always expect to see the other close behind. They were both really good at sport and well ahead of the other kids in their class. They were the only kids in their year I let play basketball against the older boys. I had been warned about Brian's illness history when he joined the school, but he had no problems. He was small but fast and full of energy.'

Brian certainly picked the right sport to be good at in Lexington. The city is the home of the University of Kentucky and its basketball team is one of the best college teams in America. They are nicknamed the Wildcats because of the bobcats which prowl the Kentucky countryside. The Wildcats have won the national championship five times, the most recent being the 1996 title, and when they play the streets of Lexington are noticeably emptier than usual. The success of the team has spawned generations of basketball mad youngsters and it's a rarity to find a house in the city without a basketball hoop attached to a side wall, or above the garage door.

Brian was one of thousands of Kentucky boys who grew up with the same dream: to be a Wildcats player. He hero-worshipped its players and when he played basketball with Chris they would adopt the name of their favourite star of the moment. They would often talk excitedly about the day, way off in the future, when they would wear the blue and white of the Wildcats and sink the winning basket in the dying seconds of a championship game. Chris says:

'Brian and I always dreamed of playing for the Wildcats. We were basketball nuts and played whenever we could. We would shoot ball until it was dark after school then continue inside with mini basket hoops in our bedrooms. Some nights at weekends we would still be playing at one or two in the morning.

'We were like brothers and spent every evening and weekend together. One weekend he would stay at my house and the next I would stay at his. Our families were really close, too, and we called each other's parents mom and dad. We were inseparable and everyone used to comment on it. We even had our own language for certain things.

'We would play sport all day long at weekends and it didn't matter to us if it was raining or snowing. We were very competitive and turned everything into a game. Usually we would play first to 100 baskets and there would never be more than a couple of shots between us. At school we would team up and play two-on-two in the playground and whenever there was a team game we made sure we were together. We hardly ever got beat because we were so much more experienced than the other kids.

'Older boys would challenge us to a game and would always underestimate us, especially Brian because he was so small. They said things like, "You're too short to play" and then he would beat them real bad.'

Being short was always a problem for Brian. He was a late developer and, even into his teens, he was far smaller than all the other guys. He believes it was something which strengthened his character and determination. 'I had a complex about being small and at times I wondered if I would ever grow. I was concerned it was something to do with all the traumas I had when I was younger. Looking back I think it helped me being a year older than the others in my class. They were maturing so much faster physically, but I could deal with being behind them because I was mentally a year ahead. Small people always have to work harder at certain things. It was tough on my self-esteem because kids would always think, Hey this little guy can't really be too good. This happened a lot in basketball and I took it as a challenge to prove myself. I was good and I had a point to prove to the bigger guys, so I made sure I won. I wouldn't back down for anybody. I would play my heart out to show them I wasn't afraid of anything and that I was a winner.'

Religion had a major influence on Brian's life and he went to church from his toddler years. His parents were committed members of their local church and brought both their sons up to be Christians. Jackie and Harold sang in the church choir and this was where young Brian learned to sing.

At first he didn't enjoy going to church. Like any young boy he wanted to play on Sundays, not get dressed up in a shirt and tie to sing hymns and say prayers. His home in Winnipeg Way backed on to the Porter Memorial Church where the family was among the most loyal in the congregation. The church had a thriving youth policy with plenty of organised activities for the youngsters, as well as the obligatory Sunday school Bible reading lessons. Brian made friends there and started to see the fun side of church and it became a major part of his social life. Chris Cawood and his family were Christians too, so Brian's new-found interest in church didn't affect their friendship.

Not surprisingly, Brian became the star player in the church basketball team and was always the one the players passed to when they needed a quick basket to win a game in the church league. He would play most Thursdays and Saturdays. For some reason, which no one seems to remember all these years later, his church pals nicknamed Brian 'Seaver', after an American baseball player called Tom Seaver.

Aside from basketball, Brian made a name for himself at Porter Memorial as one of its most promising singers. From the age of six he was recognised by choral director Ben McNees as a gifted soprano, so he encouraged and coached him. By the time he was 10, Brian was singing solos at special Christmas and Easter services and singing in the senior choir with his mother or father. One Father's Day he sang a duet with his dad.

'Singing was always something that came naturally to me. When I was a kid I heard my mom and dad sing in church and they were always practising at home. I would come in from school and the house would be filled with them singing, so I guess singing was in my blood.

'I used to sing solos in front of about 800 people in church on Sundays and it never really scared me. I always liked having a bit of attention, but I don't think I really knew what I was doing. The only acting I had done before that was in a few school plays. In church, I just got up and sang without worrying and it was quite uplifting because afterwards so many people told me how much they liked my voice.

'As I got older, I began to think about what I was doing and that's when the nerves started. When I was 13 I found it a little harder because I felt the pressure from my friends.'

Brian managed to overcome his nerves and continued as one of the church's finest singers. In the youth choir he went on tours of cities in other states with 40 or so other church kids. They had great fun travelling on coaches and staying in hostels. It was like a youth camp, but there was a serious edge to the tours. The aim was to spread the word of the Bible and bring some happiness into the lives of less privileged people. The teenagers would travel to rough parts of cities and sing in old people's residential homes, shopping malls, and give Bible readings to children in rundown schools. It was an eye-opener for Brian and he was moved by the experiences.

Ben McNees was minister of music at the church and was responsible for the New Life Choir tours. He recalls: 'Brian was a sensitive young man, with firm religious convictions, and he found a lot of the experiences on the tours very emotional. There were tears occasionally, but it was good for him and all the children to see another side to life. But we also had some great fun. Brian was a real live wire. He had a quick wit and would get everyone laughing by holding a conversation talking like Donald Duck. He was also very responsible and I could rely on him if I needed something done or one of the younger children looked after. He was elected President of the Youth Choir by his peers one year, which was quite an honour. He was only small for his age and there was a feeling amongst some of the other contenders that he wasn't up to the job, but he proved to be an excellent president. He got everyone doing their jobs and they all respected him.'

When Brian joined Tates Creek High School, his height was still a problem and it stopped him from joining the school basketball team. It was frustrating and disappointing because he was easily good enough, but there was nothing he could do about it.

His height was no problem in the school choir where he quickly proved he was head and shoulders above all the guys. His teacher, Barry Turner, had a major influence in developing Brian's voice through his teenage years and helped steer him to two successive All State Chorus line-ups, a rare achievement for a schoolboy. His success inspired confidence and raised his profile at Porter Memorial Church and within the church community of Lexington generally. By the time he was 16 he was a sought-after entertainer, booked to sing at weddings and parties. His singing activities escalated and soon after starting what would prove to be his last year at school, Brian reached a turning point which changed his views on singing.

'Singing had always been something I did in church for pleasure, but everything started to snowball. People hired me and I started getting paid to sing at weddings as a special guest, which was fantastic. I would sing three or four songs. I mostly did church songs but I also did Luther Vandross and Boyz II Men tracks. It depended on what the people wanted. Sometimes I would be paid $70, which was great money for a teenager. I also became a director of services for weddings and prepared everything in the church before the ceremony.

'I loved singing and I started working with three other guys in my high school chorus class. We messed around and sang some songs *a cappella*. A couple of the guys had dreams about becoming pop stars, but I was not really thinking along those lines. Singing had always been part of church and school to me and getting paid was just a side line that had come about by accident. I was thinking about going to college, not about becoming a singer.

'At the beginning of my junior year, when I was 17, I did a talent contest with a friend called Dawn Crumbaker. We had sung duets in church a couple of times and we decided to do a gospel song called 'Another Time, Another Place' in front of the school.

'She sang the first half of the first verse and then I came in on the second part. The moment I began singing, roars came from the audience. I couldn't have sung more than a few words and suddenly the girls were screaming. I could barely hear myself sing. I couldn't believe what was happening. Even girls I sat next to in chorus class who had heard me sing hundreds of times were screaming. Even the really popular, pretty girls were going nuts.

'I didn't realise what was going on at first. I was so nervous about singing in front of my school pals and worried about staying on pitch that my mind went blank. It was too much to take in at one time and I don't even remember the rest of the song.

'The noise from the screams and cheers at the end were awesome. It was the first time anything like that had happened to me and all I could do was turn red and smile. People certainly don't react like that when you sing in church.

'That was the first experience I ever had from really influencing an audience and it suddenly hit me that my singing could really be something for the future. I went backstage and everyone was saying, "Yeah, that was cool, Brian." It even seemed to make me more popular at school. That day really triggered something inside me.'

That something would simmer deep inside Brian for six months until Kevin's fateful call. Finally when Brian had to make the critical decision about travelling to Orlando, the adrenalin which had pumped that day in the school hall flowed back into his veins and helped him make that nerve-racking journey.

By the time Brian landed at Orlando airport the tears had dried and he felt reassured to see Kevin. He was further put at ease when he met Lou at the house.

'I had this vivid image of a businessman in a serious suit with this real Mr Important manner, but I was amazed when I met Lou. He was by the pool in his swimming trunks and a T-shirt and flip-flops. He wasn't what I expected at all. He was so cool and laid back that I felt relaxed right away. We talked a lot and I sang for him. He liked what he heard and remarked that I had a lot of gospel music in me.

'We then drove out to the Band House to meet the guys. I was pretty nervous, but AJ, Howie and Nick were very friendly. It was weird because it felt like they already knew me, even though we had just met. They immediately wanted to hear me sing, so we decided on the Boyz II Men song, 'It's So Hard To Say Goodbye' and they gave me the lead part.

'We hummed the introduction and then they started singing. When I heard them, I thought, Wow, these guys are good. It was so professional and, even though Nick was just a little kid, he had this great big voice. I was really concerned what they would think of me and I was saying to myself, Come on Brian, you've come all this way, don't mess it up now, sing well.'

He sang beautifully, and the moment Lou and the rest of the boys heard him they knew they had finally found the vital missing piece of machinery to balance the airship. Brian's voice was the perfect pitch for the five-part harmony they had been seeking. Kevin, in particular, was moved to see his cousin with the band and felt deep down that destiny had led them there.

Lou's idea had been 10 months in the making by that stage, but at last he had a talented group. The moment Brian joined is the time they all consider to be Day One of the Backstreet Boys.

8

THE POWER OF *A CAPPELLA*

Sea World is home to some of the world's most fearsome creatures. Man-eating sharks, deadly fish and its awesome performing killer whale are just some of the predatory beasts of the oceans on show at the theme park. It is one of Orlando's greatest tourist attractions and, oddly, was the venue for the Backstreet Boys' first big concert.

The boys weren't exactly being thrown to the sharks at Sea World, but in pop music terms it wasn't far off. They had been together for just two weeks since Brian joined but they already had to face their toughest test. They were to perform in the park's Nautilus Theater for 3,000 teenagers celebrating graduation night, one of the biggest parties of the social calendar for kids in America.

The gig was a *coup* for the group. It had been secured by Scott Hoekstra many weeks before, but it put severe pressure on the boys. They had performed at various restaurants, shopping malls and clubs, but this would be their first chance to sing directly for the type of audience they were aiming to capture globally. But teenagers are notoriously discerning. If they like a group, they will scream and give the best support possible. If they're not impressed, they will behave like piranha and tear the act to pieces with barracking and boos. It would be a baptism of fire for the Backstreet Boys.

The pressure on Brian was immense. His life had become a mind-spinning blur since he accepted Lou's offer. He returned to Lexington for two days with Kevin after that first trip to Orlando. He went back to Tates Creek High School and told his classmates and teachers his story and they listened in awe. Has there ever been a child who hasn't, at some point, dreamed of being able to stride into school, tell the teachers he's had enough, that he's going to be a pop star, then walk out to freedom, with his classmates cheering him like a hero? It's the kind of story which only happens in the movies, but it was unfolding in amazing Technicolor for Brian Littrell – and it was just the first scene, with the opening credits still running. He fondly remembers how his news created a buzz around the school and turned him into an instant celebrity:

'I sat in front of my chorus class and told them what had happened and they were so excited for me. They couldn't believe it. From that moment everyone seemed to look at me in a different light. It was like I had made it already. The sheer fact that I was quitting and taking the gamble made me a star.'

He had an emotional farewell with his friends at Porter Memorial church and his family. In many ways, his mum and dad were as confused as Brian. They had never imagined a future like this for their son and the ruthless, avaricious world of pop music hardly blended comfortably with their Christian ideals. But their faith told them that God had blessed their son, the boy they had nearly lost, with a wonderful talent and now it was his destiny to use it and make people happy. As Brian packed his luggage into the Bleedin' Banana and began the long drive to Orlando with Kevin, they knew he had made the right decision.

The Sea World gig was booked for Saturday, 8 May. Ironically, Brian should have been at his Junior Prom dance at Tates Creek, but instead he took centre stage with the Backstreet Boys – and what a night it was. Their nerves were frayed long before they were due to perform. Backstage, the tension was acute as Lou, Jean and Scott and the varied entourage, which was already sizeable even then, prepared the group for the big concert. They all joined hands and prayed before going on stage. The prayer would become a lasting feature of the boys' pre-concert preparation and is something they do without fail just before walking out into the spotlight.

The boys were only a short cameo slot in a variety night of entertainment, and they only sang four songs, but it was a huge step and those precious minutes on stage represented a giant leap. Scott had brought in his friend, Craig Soldinger, who was an experienced director and producer, to make a video of the show. He had three cameras in position. And it was worth recording. The audience went mad for the Backstreet Boys and the Nautilus Theater was filled with screams. The boys couldn't believe the reaction. They had individually experienced applause through their various solo efforts over the years, but this was their first taste of mania for the group. The girls particularly loved the *a cappella* style for the song, 'If I Ever Fall In Love'. It was a landmark concert and the Backstreet Boys loved every second.

'That night was awesome,' said Kevin. 'It was the first time we had played for a big audience which was really into us. We thought, Yeah, this is what it's all about. This is what we want, give us more. We came off stage on such a high. It was something I had been dreaming of for years and it all started to come into focus.'

Lou was also knocked out by the gig. 'I felt so proud when I saw them out there. I always knew we could do it but when I heard the girls screaming, it felt like everything had finally got started. Brian was great. He had only been in the group such a short time, and was only getting to know the guys, but he just went with it. No one would have guessed he'd only had a few days' rehearsals.'

It was clear at Sea World that all the parts of Lou's pop airship were in place and worked perfectly. At last it was airborne.

Everything accelerated after the Sea World concert. They were encouraged by their success and, more importantly, they felt like a solid unit for the first time. Brian had fitted in perfectly and proved himself at that gig. He sang wonderfully, worked hard at the dance routines and was an easy going guy who got on with everyone. It had never felt right with Charles and Sam, but now the Backstreet Boys really believed they had something and their small taste of audience adulation at Sea World left them hungry for more. Jean and Scott lined up as many appearances as possible to keep the momentum going. They appeared at shopping malls again, and more nightclubs and restaurants. The gigs weren't nearly as glamorous or exciting as the Nautilus Theater, but the boys needed as much varied experience as possible.

Their next prestigious gig was at a gala AIDS charity night hosted by Whitney Houston in Fort Lauderdale, a booking which had been secured after Lou donated $10,000 to the charity. It was an extravagant expense but he considered it worthwhile because it would give the boys a chance to perform in front of many celebrities and powerful people within the music business. Lou didn't expect a tangible reward from the performance, but the sheer profile of the event would help get the Backstreet Boys talked about in the right circles.

The AIDS benefit appearance was a success, but there was one unfortunate backdrop to the event. Jean Tanzy had been going through some personal difficulties in the previous months and was finding the unrelenting commitment to the group an increasing strain. That night it finally exploded, and she quit. Everyone was sad to lose her because Jean had showed unwavering belief since the earliest conception of the group. She had stepped in when Gloria Sicoli couldn't continue and had helped build the group around AJ and Howie. She had remained solid when things didn't work out with Sam and Charles and was the one who worked hard to find replacements. It seemed crazy, after all the work during the bad times, that she should quit when the good times were on the horizon. But that was her decision.

Maybe Jean could sense everything was about to move up a few gears for the Backstreet Boys. Lou now had a talented group of guys, plus a huge expenses bill, so the heat was on to turn them into stars. If anything, the pressure was about to get more intense than it had ever been in the previous 10 months. It was tough to lose someone who had been so devoted, but it was better everyone knew now, not later. After so many years in business, Lou fully expected casualties along a hard journey in search of success, so he reached a financial settlement with Jean to compensate her for all her efforts, and looked to the future.

In truth, it was a good time for the Backstreet Boys to have a new manager. They had reached a pivotal point where they were in a good position to rise up and make progress, but they were also vulnerable and could so easily sink back to the ground. They needed new ideas and fresh energy to secure a record deal. Every complex aircraft needs a skilled pilot and every successful pop group needs a capable and inspirational manager.

Gloria Sicoli proudly holds the Golden Camera Award after surprising the boys in Berlin while Denise McLean hugs Nick.

Lou Pearlman, the man they call Big Poppa, joins his "five sons" in a hotel in Sweden.

Nick dressed up in his stage
costume in crazy goggles. The
boy who was bullied at school
for wanting to sing is now flying
high as a teen superstar.

Nick relaxes in casual
clothes for a studio shot.

A rare smile from brooding Kevin.

Kevin used to sing to an empty valley but now takes centre stage with the Backstreet Boys.

Howie worked for years
trying to make it as a
child star but now
enjoys travelling the
world in the group.

Brian, the Christian choir boy from Kentucky, feels he is blessed to be able to make so many fans happy with his singing.

AJ, in his trademark sunglasses, sometimes finds fame a strain, but the thrill of performing makes it all worthwhile.

The Backstreet Boys set the stage alight as they soak up the adulation from their screaming fans.

In the spotlight. The Backstreet Boys are now the fastest growing boy band in the world.

Colourful Backstreet Boys are dressed to thrill in their stage costumes for the big European Tour of 1997.

Over the next few weeks, Lou put his mind to finding the right replacement. It seemed that Scott Hoekstra had come up with the perfect solution. Soon after Jean quit, he managed to secure a meeting with Mark Cheatham, an agent at ICM, one of the world's most powerful entertainment management agencies. The group flew to New York and impressed Cheatham with some *a cappella* songs in his office. He wanted to take them on and it seemed this was the big chance the boys had been waiting for. But then Lou got in touch with a husband-and-wife team he knew could turn his boys into superstars. They were Donna and Johnny Wright and they had all the flying skills to guide the boys to the highest altitudes in pop.

Johnny had been road manager for the New Kids on the Block and it was Johnny who introduced the Boston boys at most of the concerts. Donna and Johnny had witnessed all the hysteria, the tears and tantrums that had been whipped up around the world by the New Kids typhoon. As the New Kids faded, the Wrights started their own management company and were already developing several acts. If anyone knew about the teen pop world, it was them.

Lou sent Donna and Johnny a copy of the Sea World video. They both liked what they saw, but the sound quality was so poor they asked to hear the boys sing live. Lou told them about the long-standing arrangement where the boys sing for their dinner, so he invited them to an Italian restaurant called Carrino's in Orlando.

Donna and Johnny instantly liked the boys. They were impressed with their maturity and the depth of their show business back-grounds. The boys were in awe of the Wrights and listened intently as they recounted how they had helped the New Kids rise from obscurity to riches and stardom. As dinner ended, Donna and Johnny still hadn't said if they would represent the Backstreet Boys, but the decision was sealed when the boys stood in the middle of the restaurant and started to sing. The packed restaurant fell silent as other diners became captivated by the *a cappella* songs. Lou noticed Johnny's leg bouncing in time to the harmonies and quietly asked Donna if that was a good sign. She said, 'Yes', and added, 'If both legs start moving, it means you've got something really hot.'

By the time the boys had finished their impromptu concert, Johnny was smiling and both legs were bouncing. Sure, he wanted to be their manager.

Outside in the car park later, everyone was standing in a group saying their goodbyes when Johnny reached into his car and pulled out a present for the boys. It was a picture frame. In it was the American platinum disc of the New Kids on the Block's monster selling album, *Hangin' Tough*. It was the record which made the Boston group famous and ignited New Kids mania world-wide.

Johnny handed the frame to the boys and said: 'Put this up on the wall. Whenever you're feeling down, go and look at it. This is what the New Kids did and you can do the same. Don't think it's going to be easy because it's going to take a lot of time and a lot of sweat. It will be tough, but you have the talent to make it happen. The only time you can take this down is when you've got your own platinum album to put up in its place.'

It was a poignant moment for the Backstreet Boys and one they have never forgotten.

The platinum disc was nailed to the wall in the game room of Lou's house, which had always been the common hang-out. It was decided that if – no, *when* – they started winning awards in the future, they would all be put up on the same wall. In years to come, many more nails were hammered in as it became a jam-packed shrine to the success of the Backstreet Boys. For now, though, there were no awards remotely in sight. They weren't even close to getting a record deal, so, as the scorching heat of the summer came to Florida, it was time the Backstreet Boys started to really sweat for their success.

Donna and Johnny had plenty of ideas as to how to get the group going, but they insisted everything had to be done on their terms, by their people. This spelt the end of Scott Hoekstra's involvement. He had worked with them for free for nine months and had helped secure nearly all their early gigs and promotional appearances. But now the sights were set on an international development for the group and the Wrights already had their contacts in place. Scott was called into an office at the Kissimmee warehouse and offered compensation. It was a meeting he has never forgotten.

'I was devastated when they told me. I saw it coming when Donna and Johnny came aboard. They had their portfolio and I understood why the boys had to go with a team like that.

'I loved Lou and those guys. I would shake and cry whenever I watched them perform. I knew they could make it and I was proud to be a part of their success. I kept going because I believed in them and hoped they would keep me in the fold when things took off, but it wasn't to be.

'I didn't say anything during that meeting, but when it was over, I just said, "I did everything I promised I would do and I did it on time." I understood a tough business decision had to be taken, but it was hard to accept. I went into a deep depression after that and it lasted for two years and I've never gone back into the business. I am proud of the Backstreet Boys and happy that I played a part in getting them started. I still love them all.'

One of the first decisions the Wrights made was to take the boys on the road for a tour of schools across the States. They had done a similar Educational, Scholastic Magazines tour – or ESM – with the New Kids because it was the only way to build a fan base in the absence of a record deal and help from the media. The Wrights felt it was essential to blood the Backstreet Boys in the hard world of touring and performing for varying audiences day after day in different areas. To help develop a positive image, the band promoted an organisation represented by Kim Jacobson called SADD – Students Against Destructive Decisions – a support group aimed at helping school children to steer away from drugs and crime.

The boys hit the road in a converted coach with bunk beds – Donna and Denise McLean taking control, with Johnny and Lou joining for certain sections. They appeared at dozens of schools over the next six months, singing to pupils of all ages and audiences of all sizes, from as few as 30 to a maximum of around 400. They sang a number of songs to a backing tape of music because they had no live band. At the end of the shows they signed autographs and gave away demo tapes which included the song 'Tell Me That I'm Dreaming', which the boys had adopted as their anthem.

It was a gruelling tour, but their spirits were kept high by a predominantly positive reaction. Unfortunately, it was not always good and one appearance in Newark, New Jersey, lives in the memory of the group. The school was in a rough neighbourhood with an audience who made it clear from the start the boys weren't welcome. They were greeted with a few jeers and sarcastic whistles, which the teachers quickly stifled before they got out of hand so the Backstreet Boys could begin their act.

Just as the gig got under way the worst possible thing happened: there was a power cut. The backing tape providing the music went silent and the microphones were useless. It is every performer's worst nightmare and the Backstreet Boys were left bare and exposed. At first the crowd began to laugh: that was embarrassing. Then they started to hiss and boo: that was humiliating. The teachers tried to calm their pupils down, but it was impossible because the hecklers had safety in numbers.

The Backstreet Boys were not going to lose their nerve and cut short their act. They had covered thousands of miles, sung at dozens of venues and the experience had toughed them up. An audience might jeer at their act – that was a matter of taste – but they wouldn't put up with heckling for a technical fault beyond their control.

It was Kevin who took control. He raised his hands to appeal for quiet. At first it was ignored, but as he called out for silence the noise gradually stopped. The crowd became intrigued to see how the guy with the model looks could talk his way out of such a dire situation. In fact, Kevin wasn't going to bluff his way out of anything, he had decided the group were going to sing their way to safety. He said: 'We're sorry about the tape, but there's nothing we can do if the power goes. We've come here to sing today and that's what we're going to do. We're now going to sing you something *a cappella.*'

They began humming their way into a song and soon they were singing in wonderful harmony, the Backstreet Boys at their rawest and best. The crowd listened in stunned silence and new-found respect. These guys really could sing. The boys savoured their sweetest applause to date after that song. The taunts turned to cheers and the hall was filled with enthusiastic applause. That day they truly discovered the power of *a cappella.*

9

TIME TO GET IT GOIN'

The priority was to secure the Backstreet Boys a record deal. It sounds simple enough, but the queues to record company doors are long and full of hungry talent and always heading the lines are fast-talking managers promising their artists will be the next smash hit.

Lou and the Wrights took up the task with their normal positive determination, but even they were stunned by the reaction from the record industry. Thankfully, they didn't have to wait in line with the rest of the dreamers because they had the contacts and the track record to pass through the door to the key executives. Lou's good friend Azra Shafi helped open some doors, too. The ESM tour was interrupted several times for the boys to fly to New York, or wherever they needed to be, for meetings. The *a cappella* style was their strong selling point, so it was decided they would stand a better chance of getting a deal if the boys sang live. It was a great idea and their impromptu performances in board rooms and offices became the standard job application for the Backstreet Boys.

But it didn't do much good. The boys, Lou and the Wrights were always greeted with polite enthusiasm, mixed with a heavy dose of music biz patter, before they were ushered out of the door with promises of good news to follow. But, soon enough, the answers came back: 'Great sound, guys, but no thanks.'

The reactions were a shock. Lou could handle a few rejections and certainly hadn't expected to walk into the first record company and come out with a multi-million dollar contract. But the No pile steadily grew thicker until it included more than a dozen companies. The volume in itself was bad enough, but the recurring reason they gave seemed ominous to Lou.

'I expected it to be tough, but I was hurt when they all said No because they felt that boy bands were dead. The standard response was: "That's been done already. The New Kids burnt the whole market and it's never coming back. We want other things now."

'They also said that MTV wouldn't support us, even if we got a deal, which is vital for any record to succeed. A lot of record companies didn't even return our calls after they had seen us, which was hard to take.

'I had seen girls go crazy for the guys at Sea World and it was happening all over America on the ESM tour. The girls loved the Backstreet Boys and were screaming and banging on the bus when they showed up at the schools. I had seen all this first hand and knew it was for real, but the record company people were saying all that teen stuff was finished. I took it personally because it was like they were telling me I had read the whole situation incorrectly.'

One record company which seemed to think Lou had it right was Mercury Records. Executives in its Artists and Repertoire department – where the talent scouts work – had originally agreed to come to a school gig, but then didn't bother turning up. It had been one of many such disappointments, but Donna convinced them to change their minds. Finally veteran A&R man Dave McPherson went to a later show and instantly became a big Backstreet Boys fan. He convinced his bosses to see the boys and an *a cappella* meeting was arranged. It was a resounding success and a record contract became an administrative formality when the president of Mercury looked at the guys and confidently said: 'I feel like a Brinks security truck has just pulled up and dropped gold outside my door. We're going to do this and it's going to be awesome.'

It was the reaction everyone had dreamed of and it was a time to celebrate. The boys started thinking of their first single and then an album, a US tour. It was all going to happen, at last they were on their way. Contracts were drawn up and passed to lawyers, then suddenly, with no warning, the deal was off. Everything went belly up and Mercury pulled out. 'I couldn't believe what had happened,' says Lou. 'One minute it was on, the next it was off. I tried to contact the main guys at Mercury, but they wouldn't take my calls, so we never even got an explanation. I was so confused by it all. I wanted to know what had happened to that Brinks truck with all the gold.'

The gold treasure that was the Backstreet Boys would lie undiscovered by the record industry for many months. The Brinks truck rumbled on in the shape of a converted coach, with its bunk beds and cramped lounge area, which took the boys from school to school across America. They had been a short step from a record deal with a major player in the business, but now they were back to the daily grind. They took some comfort when Johnny and Donna told them of the countless rejections the New Kids had suffered before they finally got a break. So the Backstreet Boys swallowed their disappointment and kept on working.

Lou and Johnny kept plugging away too, and soon it seemed they had reached another breakthrough with Michael Jackson's record company. The boys flew to Los Angeles and completed another successful *a cappella* presentation. Again, it looked like it was going to happen, but the day after the meeting the child abuse allegations against Jackson were made public. The star's personal problems had a knock-on effect on his other businesses and the Backstreet Boys deal blurred into insignificance and finally vanished. It was another crushing blow.

'As disheartened as I was,' says Lou, 'I never stopped believing in the boys, not for a second. As an entrepreneur, I know you must never lose sight of the ball. You've got to keep the original vision in your mind and don't let it go, no matter how many disappointments. If you truly believe in something enough, you stick with it and it will work. I have grown used to rejections and I know, if you keep shopping and go to a hundred places, you'll get a break in the end.'

That break finally came in early 1994 when Jeff Fenster and David Renzer from Zomba/Jive Records saw the boys perform in Cleveland,

Ohio. Soon after, Barry Weiss and Fenster discussed the boys with Dave McPherson who had joined Jive and they decided to take on the group. The deal was signed in New York and Lou threw a big party to celebrate. At last the bullion truck had a home and could start unloading its precious cargo.

Getting a record contract was a huge relief for the Backstreet Boys, but it signalled the start of the really hard graft. Now that they had a big company working full out to break them, the pace quickened considerably. Jive were pleased with the groundwork the group had already done on the ESM tour and an assortment of other gigs but, as far as they were concerned, the surface had hardly been scratched. They wanted the Backstreet Boys to develop a considerable fan base across America long before they started recording material in the studio. There was no way Jive would go to the expense of producing a single in the simple hope that it would be bought cold. That would be business suicide and no good for anyone, least of all the boys.

Apart from the business equations, it was also better for the Backstreet Boys not to be rushed. They were still relatively raw and needed more time to develop their image and their act. The New Kids on the Block had failed with their first album because they hadn't laid down the necessary foundations. It had been a hard lesson to learn and one the Wrights remembered well because it had nearly been a fatal blow. Jive were determined not to take the same risk with the Backstreet Boys. The boys had a lot to learn and needed to be as polished as possible when it came for the big launch. So for the next year they worked on every aspect of the group. They sweated in the dance studio with top choreographers and spent hours with photographers and stylists. Above all, they sang together and worked endlessly on new material and their harmonies. Only then did they embark on another tour of the States. They clocked up many more thousands of miles across the length and breadth of the country, performing in more schools and clubs and for the music and teen press.

As if they didn't have enough to do preparing the group for world success, Brian, AJ and Nick had yet to graduate from high school, and Howie was still studying for his art degree. They had studied continuously with tutors since the group started, so Brian was able to return briefly to Tates Creek to graduate with his school buddies and Howie passed his degree. Eventually AJ and Nick would also pass their school exams.

Their education in the pop world continued as they followed an exhausting path of travelling and performing. There were few signs of the so-called glamour of stardom which most of them had dreamed of when they were younger. Sure, they were greeted like heart throbs at some schools and begged for autographs, so they began to feel a little bit like stars, but predominantly life on the road was an endurance test with few trimmings.

Gradually, it began to pay off as their stage act tightened and their harmonies blended more sweetly. They steadily became more professional and slick and soon the seedy nightclubs and small schools in the back of beyond were no longer necessary. They were good enough for bigger audiences and they were lined up as a support act in arenas to open for famous groups such as the Village People and REO Speedwagon. It was a major step for the Backstreet Boys, the pop stars of the future, to support the heroes of yesteryear.

As the months wore on, Jive were busy planning the future. They were scheduling the assault on the music business and scouting for the right producing and writing talent to link up with the Backstreet Boys. Jive had many options, but, as they saw the boys develop, they decided the best suited was Denniz PoP, a Swedish musician who had written a string of hits for chart groups, including Ace of Base. Denniz had a number of new songs ready to record, but there was one in particular he felt would be perfect for Jive's new boy band. It was a thumping, energetic track he had written with his partners Max Martin and Herbert Crichlow. It was called 'We've Got It Goin' On'.

Jive thought it was perfect too and, in the summer of 1995, the Backstreet Boys flew to Sweden to record the single at Cheiron Studios in Stockholm. They clicked so well with Denniz and his team that they prolonged their stay to record two more songs, 'Nobody But You' and 'Quit Playing Games (With My Heart)'. They all got an amazing buzz when they heard those tracks played back. That feeling was matched back in Orlando when they shot the video to the song and the first copies of the CD were delivered, complete with cover and case. Now it felt like they were in a pop group, not a cabaret act which only performed in small clubs to partially interested audiences. After all the months of hard work, they were finally getting goin'.

'We've Got It Goin' On' was released across America in August with a blast of promotion orchestrated by Jive. It climbed to No. 69 and had all the potential to have a healthy life, growing stronger up the charts. But the Backstreet Boys' first delivery was abandoned soon after its arrival. The teen magazines were kind enough, but the wider music press wouldn't write about it, most radio stations hardly played it and MTV, the midwife to all mainstream pop and rock music in America, strangled it at birth by refusing to screen the video. Only The Box played the video. All the plans for a promotional tour of the States to boost the single had to be scrapped. What was the point in promoting a single no one could hear? Predictably, it vanished from the Top 100. The words from the doom merchants who had turned the group away, warning they wouldn't get the support they needed, came back to haunt everyone. It was more than two years since Lou had dispatched Gloria Sicoli to find the best young talent in Florida. After everything the boys had done, after all the money he had spent, was this all they were going to get?

A DJ called Hildie on XL 106.7 FM in Orlando was one of the few who supported 'We've Got It Goin' On' and the boys have always been eternally grateful. She had heard about the group through a hard core of fans who had followed the boys since Sea World. They kept ringing Hildie requesting the song, so she put it on her play list, but her efforts were an inaudible squeak in a deep canyon. The Backstreet Boys needed to make a big noise to stand any chance of being heard in America, but they had been muzzled. 'We've Got It Goin' On' had some success in the dance music chart after a re-mix version became popular in nightclubs, but that market was not important to the group. It was all very depressing and worrying. During this time the boys' spirits hit an all time low during a gig at a club in Miami called Amnesia. It was a night they all consider their worst and one they would rather forget. Nick recalls:

'We got a bad vibe from the moment we arrived at the club. It was full of older guys who were partying pretty hard. They were mostly black guys and Hispanics, so a young white group of boys looked pretty out of place. We weren't too worried about playing there because we were positive about any place we got a chance to sing. But the problems started when the announcer went on stage. He was meant to introduce us, but he made a mistake and said the wet T-shirt competition was next. Everyone started cheering and whistling, then the guy realised his mistake. He said, "Err, sorry guys, the next act is the Backstreet Boys."

'We went out on stage and of course the guys were going crazy. They were expecting to see some beautiful girls and instead they got a bunch of young white kids. They were booing and jeering. We'd never come across that before so it was quite a shock.

'We started singing but they kept booing us, which was hard to deal with. We had to grit our teeth and get on with it. They were shouting out all kinds of things at us while we were singing. They just wanted to see some girls. It was an uncomfortable atmosphere and we couldn't wait to finish and get out that club. We were pretty upset that night.'

The European launch of the single came a month or so later – and suddenly the depression lifted. Boy bands may have been dead in America, but they were as hot as ever on the Continent. Take That – minus Robbie Williams – were still the undisputed kings and Boyzone were emerging as the young pretenders to the throne. A plethora of other boy groups surrounded the big two, but this didn't stop the Backstreet Boys making an impression. News soon reached them that 'We've Got It Goin' On' was climbing the charts in Germany, so Jive told the boys to abandon America for now and go where they were wanted.

They were greeted in Germany as stars. It was an amazing turnaround considering the disastrous launch in the States, and that first visit to Germany marked the earliest days of what would snowball into Backstreet Boys mania there. It was the big opening the boys had been longing for and now the doors which had been closed were flung wide open and the red carpets were rolled out. They were invited on to all the main music TV shows, interviewed by the teen magazines, and were special guests at the Popcorn Party, Germany's prime teen pop event. 'We've Got It Goin' On' was in the top 10 and they were awarded their first Gold Disc. Later the boys and Lou would nail it to the wall right next to the New Kids' platinum album in what would become an emotional ritual every time they received a landmark award.

The wave of interest in Germany caused ripples in other European countries and it wasn't long before interest picked up in Britain. The boys held a launch party for the single in Britain at Planet Hollywood and impressed even cynical pop journalists who had grown punch drunk with boy bands. Despite winning the press over, the single didn't break into the Top 40, but their promotion work, including a slot on *Live and Kicking*, earnt the boys an invitation to join the Smash Hits Roadshow, the chief showcase for a teen group wanting to succeed in Britain. It was a vital breakthrough and the Backstreet Boys proved themselves worthy of the invite by winning the Best New Tour Act Award at the Smash Hits Poll Winners' Party.

It was one of the highlights of a turbulent and confusing year. The Backstreet Boys' airship had been inexplicably grounded at home, but across the Atlantic it had started to soar.

10

STREETS OF GOLD

The volume of work which faced the Backstreet Boys in 1996 was mind-boggling. The focus was Europe, particularly Germany, with excursions to the Far East and Canada. Now they had prised open the all-important first door in Germany, they had to knock on as many others as soon as possible to maintain the momentum. Plans were in place for the release of several more singles and to record their debut album. It would be an exhausting year of virtually non-stop travelling, performing and recording.

The release of 'I'll Never Break Your Heart' in Britain was a flop and only managed to reach No. 42. But fan mania in Germany was proving unbreakable and thanks to Johnny Wrights tour promotion contacts David Zedeck and Werner Lindinger, the Backstreet Boys were welcomed as a support group for established bands, such as Caught in the Act and DJ Bobo, which gave the boys the chance to show big audiences what they could do. The girls loved the moving *a cappella* ballads and the intensity of the live singing. It was clear the boys weren't using computer enhanced backing tapes, a trick so often used by young groups; they could really sing and their style hit a nerve which made the Backstreet Boys the buzz band in Germany.

It was not long before they had enough fans of their own to give up the support act work and begin an independent tour of Germany. It was a sell-out and the boys started to experience the first signs of hysteria which would follow them everywhere in the country and, eventually, all over Europe. The success in Germany seemed to be reaching Britain when the third single, 'Get Down', reached No. 14, and gave them a coveted appearance on *Top Of The Pops*. Now their following in Britain was starting to grow.

'It was amazing how fast everything happened,' says Lou. 'One day we were down about the single in America, but the next the boys had thousands of fans screaming at them. It was very exciting to see it all unfold and we knew it was just the beginning.'

During a break from touring and promoting, they returned to Orlando to record the rest of the material for their debut album. As they prepared the cover, the boys penned their thanks to everyone who had helped them over the years. They all underlined their faith in God and their appreciation of Donna and Johnny Wright and, above all, they acknowledged Big Poppa Lou for his constant support and belief.

Poignantly, Kevin made a moving tribute to his father. It read: 'On August 26 1991, I lost my father to cancer. He was the greatest man I'll ever know. If I can be half the man you were as a father, a husband and as a friend, then I will consider myself to be successful. I miss you dad. I dedicate this album to my father, Jerald Wayne Richardson.' The tragedy that his father cannot share in his success still deeply hurts Kevin and the pain is compounded the further the group progress. 'If I had one wish it would be for my father to come back,' he says.

Once the album was finished, the boys were back on the seemingly endless round of promotion work and appearances in Europe, the Far East, and especially Canada, where an enthusiastic following was also starting to develop. All the ground work showed dividends when the album was released and it became an instant hit in more than a dozen countries, including Thailand, Korea, Spain and all of Scandinavia. But it was in Germany that it proved to be the biggest success and earned the Backstreet Boys their first platinum album for 500,000 sales. They were not quite up there with the New Kids, but it was the right colour disc and an amazing leap forward, not to mention another space of Lou's wall beautifully decorated. Besides, *Hangin' Tough* had been the New Kids' second album. This was the Backstreet Boys' first.

The single 'We've Got It Goin' On' was re-released in Britain on 18 August. This time it was a hit and climbed to No. 3, sparking good sales of the album, too. At last Britain was catching up with the mania across the rest of Europe, so the boys announced their first major tour. It included 14 dates in November, mainly at theatres and medium-sized arenas, but before that they crammed in a whirlwind tour of South East Asia, including Hong Kong, Singapore, Malaysia, the Philippines, Japan and Australia. Word even came through that their songs were sparking interest in South America. It seemed every country outside North America wanted to listen to the Backstreet Boys.

The British tour was a success and it helped take the re-release of 'I'll Never Break Your Heart' to No. 8. Although the venues on the tour were not sell-outs, the sheer volume of fans proved that the Backstreet Boys had truly broken the British market. After the final night in Brighton, it was decided that the next tour of the UK would be their full arena extravaganza which they had taken across Germany.

One of the final highlights of 1996 came during the MTV Europe Awards. The Backstreet Boys were not expecting to win any awards. They were still relatively new on the scene and were up against some huge acts like Oasis, Boyzone and the runaway sensation of the year, the Spice Girls. But, against the odds, the boys won Europe's Best Group Award after a phone-in poll. It was an incredible way to finish a sensational year.

Back in Orlando in early 1997, the boys relaxed and caught up with their families while working in the studio on new material. The primary task for the year ahead was to move on to the next level in all the countries where they had succeeded, with bigger tours and more hits. But, above all, they aimed to crack America.

The plan for the States was to cut a new album with a blend of tracks from the debut disc and the best of their new songs, then commit themselves to a huge promotion campaign. The feedback from the record industry in America showed that maybe this time round the Backstreet Boys would stand a better chance of success, thanks to having already proved themselves in Europe and the world by selling 8.5 million CDs.

While in Florida working on the new album, AJ had an unexpected emotional reunion with his dad, whom he had not seen or heard from since he was 10. It happened when he came across a court document sent to his grandparents referring to a Robert McLean. It had an address in Orlando and he couldn't resist checking it out. AJ tells the story.

'I was curious to see if he was really at that address, so a friend picked me up and we drove over. There were no cars outside the house, but I knocked on the door and this guy answered. I was 10 the last time I saw my dad, so I had no idea what he would look like, so I asked him, "Are you Robert McLean?"

'He took one look at me and knew who I was. He gave me a big hug and started crying. It was really weird and emotional meeting him again. I went inside and met my step-mother. It turned out that he had been living in Orlando for a few years, not far from me.

'We had a good chat. He knew all about the Backstreet Boys, even though we weren't famous in America. He had bought our album from an import CD store and had read all the teen magazine interviews with me and the guys. He had followed us on the Internet and knew my tour schedule. It was crazy to think he knew so much about me, but I knew nothing about him.

'I flat out asked him why he never called or wrote to me. He said he didn't get in touch because he thought I didn't want anything to do with him. He thought my mom and my grandparents had put things into my head that he was this evil and terrible person who never wanted to see his son.

'I told him that wasn't true. No one ever talked about him, it was like he didn't exist, so I wasn't fed bad things about him. I told him I was cool about everything and that I didn't blame him, or anybody for what had happened. My mom and dad were just not meant to stay together.

'He came down to meet all the guys during a photo shoot and they thought he was cool. He is a real hippie kind of guy, with long hair, and is so excited that we are together again. He's like a big kid and wants to hang out a lot, but it's difficult because I am not around much these days. We are slowly building a relationship and he pages me all the time.'

Soon after AJ found his dad, he had to say goodbye again to go back on the road with the Backstreet Boys. They spent a week rehearsing in Belgium for what would be their biggest tour to date. It would feature a full live band and take them on 37 dates across France, Scandinavia, Germany and Canada.

Just before the first night on 7 February, they flew to Berlin to pick up a Golden Camera Award where they met a special guest. Movie superstar Arnold Schwarzenegger headlined the celebrity list at the ceremony. When he saw all the screaming fans, he said to the boys: 'I guess all these girls aren't here for me.' The fact that they were hanging out with Arnie was an indication of the Backstreet Boys' growing status, but the muscle-bound actor was not the star of the show for them that night. It was a woman no-one knew: Gloria Sicoli.

Lou and the Wrights had arranged for Gloria to surprise the boys and present them with their latest award. She was introduced by the presenter. Sadly, the introduction was in German, so she had no idea what was being said, but it would have been along the lines that this was the woman who helped find the Backstreet Boys. Gloria basked in her first taste of recognition for her work outside the tight circle of friends who knew about her involvement. 'It was a fantastic night,' she says. 'The boys had no idea I was going because I haven't been well enough to travel for a long time.

'Howie and AJ were wonderful. They hugged me and introduced me to everyone. I was so pleased to see them and it was great to get to know Kevin and Brian and Nick.

'The fans were going crazy for the guys and it was amazing to think it all started with me doing those ads and going through the archives in the Civic Theater. I feel very proud to have played a small part in it, but it is Lou who has made it all happen. It was his dream and if it wasn't for him, no one would have a job.'

As the Backstreet Boys began their marathon European tour, news came back from Britain that 'Quit Playing Games (With My Heart)' had reached No. 15. Compared with their success on the Continent this was nothing to cheer about, but they quickly improved their UK chart standing with their next release the following month. They jetted back from Germany to sing 'Anywhere For You' on the midweek *Lottery Live* show. It certainly gave the song a boost and helped send it straight to No. 4. Unfortunately, they weren't to scoop the jackpot with that song climbing to the very top, but surely their first UK No. 1 couldn't be far off.

In four helter-skelter years the lives of all the Backstreet Boys have changed beyond recognition. They now have fame and hits in more than 20 countries and their popularity grows daily. They are all coping well with the pressures of pop stardom, but there are many downs as well as ups on their crazy roller-coaster ride. They certainly find life on the road draining and often monotonous.

Kevin says: 'Life on the road is a lot harder than I ever imagined and it's nothing like as glamorous as people think. Seeing this life has given me even more respect for all my favourite artists like Elton John and Prince. To be at the top of this business for so long is an incredible achievement. There is so much work to do and you have to eat, drink and sleep the job. That's what we are doing and it's paying off. I couldn't take this life forever and eventually I want to be a writer and producer for other people. That way, I can have a family and a regular home.'

Brian says: 'I honestly feel I am blessed and that God gave me this gift to sing for a reason. I believe he left me on earth after I was so ill as a kid so that somehow I can bless others, not necessarily religiously or by talking about God, but by just making someone feel good. If I smile at fans from the stage, they grin from ear to ear and to be able to make someone happy and influence their lives positively gives me a great sense of fulfilment inside. It's an awesome feeling.'

Nick certainly feels the strain of stardom. 'I love the entertainment part of this business,' he says, 'but I find everything else hard. I miss home and my family badly. It's so pretty and relaxing where I live, but I am so rarely there. Being famous is very stressful and a lot of people don't realise how hard we work. We are up at the crack of dawn most days, travel all day, then perform at night. That's the schedule day after day and you feel so tired. But the bad parts even out because we get such a buzz from performing and we meet some great people.'

Howie says: 'I thought being a pop star would be so easy. I thought you would lay in bed all day, hang out, do a show and have a great party all night. But the reality is much harder. I didn't realise how many press and photo shoots you would have to do. But it's a life I dreamed of and I enjoy the travelling and I love the fans.

'The guys call me "Sweet D" because I can never say No to the fans. They're fantastic and keep us going when we're down. I'm always the last on the bus because I'm waving and signing autographs. It drives our security guys crazy and they keep saying that one day they'll drive off too soon by mistake and I'll be carried away by the fans.

'I have also started to realise how important the business side of things is. Out of all the guys, I tend to be the one who makes sure we're not spending too much money. You hear so many bad stories about young guys blowing opportunities, but we have a chance to do well from all this work, so we must not mess it up. We are starting to earn some money now because our tours are getting bigger. Personally, I want to invest what I earn so all the work pays off in the future.'

AJ, the first Backstreet Boy, is revelling in the band's success.

'Over the past couple of years everything has grown slowly, but now it grows a huge amount every day. When I look at a list of our record sales around the world it blows me away. We are going gold in places we haven't even visited yet and you think, Hey, this is crazy.

'It's hard work, but I'm loving every minute. It has its ups and downs and you go through all kinds of emotions. Sometimes I can't cope and I break down. I have cried in my room from being lonely and wanting to be home. I have thought, I can't do this anymore, please let me be a regular kid and not a Backstreet Boy anymore. Sometimes I just wish I was at college or in a regular job with a normal life.

'It's the little things that get to you. I love McDonald's food and used to eat it all the time, but I can't walk out and grab a burger these days. I have to go with security looking over me and sometimes I wish I could live my life normally.

'But when you're on stage and you see the fans, that's when

we know why we're doing this and why we wouldn't want to be doing anything else. It's the most amazing feeling and the biggest high you can get. You forget about all the travelling, the long hours, the interviews, and do the show and listen to the fans.

'The fans love the shows because we have talent and give it everything we've got. We dance and put on an act for them, but they know we can sing anything at the drop of a hat. It is a God-given talent and we use it to the best of our ability.

'We are trying to establish ourselves as all-round musicians. I have started playing the bass, Howie and Brian are playing guitar, Kevin already plays piano and Nick plays the heck out of the drums. Soon we plan to play 'Quit Playing Games' totally by ourselves and get the band to do the dancing!

'Our shows are getting bigger and better, but no matter how big we get we will always be at our best when we have five open mikes and we sing *a cappella*, that's when you have the Backstreet Boys. Those harmonies will keep us in tune with our roots.'

As for Lou Pearlman, the man with the master plan, these are amazing times. His aviation empire still thrives and he runs it skilfully, but these days he is not rooted to his Orlando office. He is more often found in his Planet Hollywood bomber jacket and jeans, orchestrating deals from a phone backstage at a Backstreet Boys concert, or an airport lounge thousands of miles from home. He is never happier than when he is jetting around the world with his boys. He is not quite the rock star he yearned to be, but he's pretty close. As the sixth Backstreet Boy, the fans swarm round him in hotel lobbies, ask for his autograph and take his picture. He loves it.

'For me, this is the most exciting thing I've ever done because it's about people, not machines. Airships are great, but they only hum, they don't sing and laugh.

'I have been with the boys during many tough times and helped them through. I've seen them when they were down, and laughed with them when things were great. It has been like raising kids and now I'm enjoying watching them succeed and having the time of their lives.

'I think we are going to stay in the business longer than the New Kids because the boys are more dedicated to making music. Obviously, they will need to make it big in America first and the boys, Jive, the management team and I will try our best to make that happen.

'The best thing for me has been the family which has grown with the Backstreet Boys. We talk deeply about what is happening to them and where we are going. We make sure everyone is in check and coping OK. Nothing has gone to anyone's head and, like all good families, we are always supportive.

'I get a buzz watching the girls scream at the guys and I get a thrill from the music. Being a part of all this makes me feel very lucky. There is an energy that comes off the boys when they walk into a room and it's a great feeling. I love these boys like they are my own kids and I couldn't imagine having five better sons.'

When you travel with the Backstreet Boys you get to see that family atmosphere up close. Despite the fatigue and pressurised schedule, there is still a constant brotherly banter between the boys and their personal bodyguards. Denise McLean is a critical part of the team. She is the tour Mama who works continuously to keep the boys happy and busy and she means it when she hugs Lou backstage and says: 'This is a family which was destined to be together.'

Without fail, the whole team pray together a few minutes before the boys go on stage. Everyone is called out of various dressing rooms by the booming words from Randy Jones, the head of security – 'Okay, everybody, let's pray.'

The five boys, their musicians, the principal security men, Denise and Lou all hold hands and form a circle. Randy selects someone and they say a prayer for everyone. It is not a rehearsed set piece, but a general thanks to God for the boys' talent, everyone's health, their success and for the fans. During the prayer, anyone not in the tight circle stands like a statue in the corridor.

Once the prayer is finished, the boys launch straight into another, more jocular ritual which lightens the serious tone. Randy wishes them well with a simple parting comment like, 'Have a good one, guys' and all five Backstreet Boys shout back *'Hey, Negro, that's all you had to say! We're outta here!'* The skit is a parody of a scene from *Pulp Fiction*, the movie they all loved during the 1996 tours. No matter how many times they do it, they all laugh and are still smiling as they walk into the darkness and follow narrow flashlight beams to the stage.

The scenes that greet the Backstreet Boys are the same in arenas around the world – mind-spinning hysteria. Screams from thousands of girls pierce the ears, hundreds of fluorescent necklaces spin in the darkness, banners proclaim undying love for one or all the boys, and roses, furry toys, and other, more personal, items are thrown at their feet.

To witness a Backstreet Boys concert from the pit – the section between the foot of the stage and the barrier holding back the first row of fans – is a truly intoxicating experience. It is a place reserved for security men, the in-house video camera crew and, basically, Lou Pearlman and his guest. There you feel the full convergence of the energy from the boys and the hysteria from the fans. It is a place where the reality of the Backstreet Boys' incredible success story comes into sharp focus.

Looking a few feet forward you can see every facial expression on each of the guys. You can see the intense concentration in their eyes, the sweat on their brows, the stress on their throats from singing, and the sheer physical exertion of each choreographed dance step.

Looking a few feet back is the response to those exhaustive efforts. Thousands of girls' faces show a range of undiluted emotions. They are sobbing with tears streaming down flushed cheeks, some are singing, some are screaming maniacally and many are simply starring open-mouthed. Every now and then one startled fan will break into uncontrollable screams as she locks eye contact with one of the boys for a fleeting moment.

In scenes reminiscent of all the great acts which have sparked mania, from The Beatles to the Osmonds, to the New Kids and Take That, girls scream themselves to a state of delirium and collapse. Every few minutes, security men dash through the pit. One guard jumps on a chair, dives forward until he is submerged beneath the first few rows of young faces. Other men desperately hold his jeans belt, until he emerges seconds later clutching a limp girl, her face red and her hair damp. Half conscious, she is carried to the side of the stage; her Backstreet Boys experience is over, but never forgotten. This rescue act is repeated dozens of times throughout the concert while the boys continue to sing and dance.

The hysteria surrounding the group is all the more amazing when you look back on the boys' lives and consider their journeys to the spotlight. So much has happened since they performed in school plays, sang in talent contests and church choirs, faced countless rejections, and even sang to the animals in tree-lined valleys.

In four years, the Backstreet Boys have gone from dreaming nobodies to pop superstars with the world at their feet. No one can doubt that AJ, Howie, Nick, Kevin and Brian are talented performers who have worked hard for their success and deserve every scream, dollar and teeny-bopper tear. That *Hangin' Tough* platinum disc still hangs on the wall in Orlando, but for how much longer? Only a few barriers stand between the boys and worldwide success and surely the only direction now for the soaring Backstreet Boys airship is UP.

It began with a throwaway conversation with Art Garfunkel and became the dream of a man in search of a family and a rock 'n' roll fantasy. Lou Pearlman dreamed it and knew he could make it happen. Now he beams with pride in the pit as his five boys live the dream.

ABOUT THE AUTHOR

Rob McGibbon began his journalistic career on the *Wimbledon News*, in south London, and worked as a news reporter and show business writer on several national newspapers before leaving to write books.

In 1990, he co-wrote the first biography of the New Kids on the Block with his father, Robin, also a journalist. They gambled on publishing the book themselves, before the band were famous in Britain, and it became a worldwide bestseller. In the next three years, they wrote biographies of England footballer Paul Gascoigne, TV presenter Phillip Schofield and Simply Red's lead singer Mick Hucknall. In addition, Rob wrote a biography of Take That, which was a bestseller in Germany, *Boyzone on the Road* for Boxtree, and the forthcoming *Boyzone, The True Story*.

Between writing books, Rob is a freelance journalist writing mainly celebrity interviews for newspapers and international magazines. He lives in Chelsea, London. Among his many interests is soccer and, as a life-long Chelsea fan, one of his proudest moments was playing in a celebrity match at Stamford Bridge.